FOLLOW ME

A Memoir in Challenges

B
DILLON, R.
D

RICKY DILLON

Keywords

PRESS

—

ATRIA

NEW YORK   LONDON   TORONTO   SYDNEY   NEW DELHI

ATRIA PAPERBACK
An Imprint of Simon & Schuster, Inc.
1230 Avenue of the Americas
New York, NY 10020

First Keywords Press/**ATRIA** PAPERBACK edition June 2016

KEYWORDS PRESS/**ATRIA** PAPERBACK and colophons are trademarks of
Simon & Schuster, Inc.

For information about special discounts for bulk purchases, please
contact Simon & Schuster Special Sales at 1-866-506-1949 or
business@simonandschuster.com.

The Simon & Schuster Speakers Bureau can bring authors to your
live event. For more information or to book an event, contact the
Simon & Schuster Speakers Bureau at 1-866-248-3049 or
visit our website at www.simonspeakers.com.

Interior design by Kyoko Watanabe

Manufactured in the United States of America

10 9 8 7 6 5 4 3 2 1

Library of Congress Cataloging-in-Publication Data is available.

ISBN 978-1-5011-3201-8
ISBN 978-1-5011-3202-5 (ebook)

I dedicate this book to all of my incredible fans, who have supported me endlessly. You're all the reason why I do what I do, and everything I do is for you. Thank you for continuing to inspire me every single day. You're my biggest motivation and I can never thank you enough. I love you all so much! This book is for you.

FOLLOW ME

INTRODUCTION

Hey, guys, what's up!

Do you ever wonder which YouTuber said that first? Whoever it was should have trademarked the phrase, seeing as how 98 percent of us now use that same line to kick off a video. The person would be filthy rich by now!

Or not. What's so cool about YouTubers is that I don't think many of us would ever be that stingy. The beautiful thing about YouTube is that it's all about sharing! Collaborating and group participation are what we thrive on, and in that spirit, this book that you're holding in your hands is not just me telling a bunch of little stories about my life. It's also a chance for us to do some fun stuff together.

It's a pretty simple concept—each section within each chapter has a challenge that's related to the subject I'm writing about, along with an extra totally random challenge thrown in for good measure! I'm going to be doing every single one of them, and you should do them along with me! If you complete one, put a photo or video of it on Twitter, Instagram, Tumblr, or YouTube with the hashtag #FOLLOWMEBOOK, along with the hashtag assigned to each individual challenge. I'll check it out and then repost it! Plus I'll be posting my favorites along the way on my YouTube channel.

When I first came up with the idea of doing a book, I knew I didn't want to put something out that people would read and then place on their shelf to gather dust over the next ten years. I wanted something readers could keep coming back to, so I divided everything up by theme. This way if you ever find yourself in the mood to make a big change in your life, go back to the Ambition chapter and read my story on Self-Empowerment. Or if one day you're feeling sad for any reason, flip to the Bummed Out chapter and check out the Social section. The whole point is to make this a different experience for everyone who picks it up. You'll learn stuff about my family and my YouTube friends as well as my personal ones, along with my worries, insecurities, greatest memories, and tons more. Most important, I hope that by doing the challenges you'll learn something new about yourself, too.

Ready? Let's do this!

CHAPTER 1

HAPPY

CHALLENGE

#DYEFORRICKY

Dye your hair a crazy, wild color. It
doesn't have to be permanent—there are
tons of temporary options out there.

SOCIAL

.

Here's something you don't hear too often: I was a happy kid growing up. My home life was awesome. I had parents who adored me and an older sister named Tara whom I was obsessed with because she never treated me like a bratty younger brother, and between band, tennis, and a job at the mall, my life was pretty full.

We lived in Hoover, Alabama, a large, safe suburb of Birmingham. My dad worked as a pharmaceutical rep, Mom was a homemaker, and in high school I had a bright orange Kia Soul and a best friend named Shelby who was always up for anything. So it wasn't like I was trying to escape some sort of horrible existence when I first started to meet people and make new friends on YouTube.

I actually have Miley Cyrus to thank for my discovery of the site. More specifically, Hannah Montana. I was obsessed with the show. Not just for its kooky secret identity plot lines—I legitimately loved the music they played on it. I couldn't find the songs on iTunes, though, and the Disney Channel hadn't released any CDs yet because the show had just debuted. What can I say, I'm an early adopter.

I hit Google up to see if I could find anyone who had uploaded the music to stream, and that's when I stumbled across YouTube. Not only did I find all the songs from the show there, but people had posted lyric videos, too, so I could sing along. (My favorite was the song "This Is the Life.") The website seemed cool, but there was no immediate feeling of OMG THIS IS MY FUTURE CALLING.

A few years later, Ke$ha's song "Tik Tok" came out, and I loved it. I went back to YouTube to look for the video after hearing it on the radio so I could listen to it as many times as I wanted. That's when I discovered that tons of people were doing parody videos of it. I quickly became obsessed, and loved watching so many different kids offer their own take on the ridiculously catchy song. I was cruising through a whole stream of parodies on YouTube when I clicked on one by a girl named Braeton Brescia, who went by the username SoCalhco888. I started watching a bunch of her videos and thought they were hilarious, and through the recommended "up next" list that runs along the side of the YouTube screen, I discovered more YouTubers, like iJustine, Smosh, Brittani Louise Taylor, Andrea Russett, and a guy named Shane Dawson. He was singing along to "Tik Tok" on the radio in a car, so he hadn't technically done a parody video, but he seemed really funny so I watched another one of his clips. And then another. And then another.

Maybe two hours went by before I came up for air. Here's the thing—even though I had some really solid friends, I was pretty sheltered. I didn't go to parties and no one in my circle was particularly wild. Watching YouTubers like Shane, I felt like I'd suddenly made new friends who said all of the crazy, insane things that everyone thinks about inside, but doesn't have the guts to say out loud. I couldn't believe that this world existed and I'd never known about it. Actually I'm pretty sure no one in Alabama aside from me even knew what YouTube was at that point.

I still had my old account from back in the days when I used to watch Hannah Montana videos, but I'd only ever used it to save videos I liked. I noticed that there seemed to be these whole micro-communities within the comments sections, and that the YouTubers themselves would sometimes even join the conversation. I started leaving little comments of my own, and would be thrilled and shocked when someone replied to something I wrote, or gave my messages a thumbs-up.

YouTube was a whole new way of communicating with the world. I'd lived in the same town my entire life and knew what to expect from everyone around me. There were no surprises. Suddenly the entire globe seemed to explode before my eyes, and it all revolved around these funny, weird goofballs. There was something about the way they acted on camera—totally without shame or embarrassment—that looked so freeing. I couldn't fathom acting like they did out in the real world, but I felt like I shared the same sense of humor as these people, and the idea of acting as crazy as I wanted, showing my creativity and self-expression without being scared that someone would make fun of me, suddenly seemed like a really important goal to chase. I had to let myself go and show my true self, something I had never really done before.

I got Shelby into watching YouTubers with me and she loved them as much as I did, so we decided to start our own channel. My nickname at the time was Pickle, owing to the fact that my last name is Dillon. (As in *dill* pickle. Get it?) Shelby's nickname was Banana, but only because some random girl started calling her that one day. So we named our channel PICKLEandBANANA.

Quick side note about P&B: I can't stand the name now.

I feel like I have to explain the origin all the time because so many dirty-minded people thought it had something to do with, well, you know. It was very innocent, though! I swear!

Anyway, we did a few music parodies. I knew how to use a video camera since I'd always made home movies when I went on vacation with my family. Even though I could be shy in real life, I always came alive in front of a camera. I directed Shelby and myself singing and dancing around to Britney Spears, Black Eyed Peas, and Aaron Carter. Unfortunately she got kind of bored with it all because her schedule was already really busy and it usually took all day to make just one video.

I continued to watch videos in my free time over the next few months, and slowly began itching to get back involved. I kept commenting on my favorite YouTubers' videos and started to amass a whole new social circle online. I loved my friends from school, but I got something different from these people. They felt more directly in line with the way my brain worked.

It felt a little creepy telling my parents, "Hey, look at all these new friends I made on the internet!" But since they were on YouTube, I could actually see their faces, so I knew that I was messaging with a guy or girl my own age who genuinely had the same interests as me. As opposed to some pervy old dude hiding behind a fake screen name, pretending to be a fourteen-year-old girl.

I set up my Ricky Dillon channel at exactly the right time— I'm part of the lucky first wave that got into YouTube early, back when making friends with strangers on the site was much easier than it is now. At that time, there were only a handful of megastars, and they engaged a lot more directly with fans by hosting video contests. You could easily upload your video to their video response section (which sadly doesn't exist anymore), and if they liked you best you'd get a special shout-out, which introduced you to all of their subscribers.

I have Braeton and her SoCalhco888 channel to thank for my first few thousand subscribers, which are always the hardest to get. I entered two of her contests with music videos of "Tik Tok" and "Starstrukk" by 3OH!3, and I placed really high both times!

In that same spirit, the first themed challenge to kick-start this book not only brings back that tradition but encourages you to reach out and make a new friend.

CHALLENGE

#FRIENDFINDERFORRICKY

Reach out to someone you've never met before but know has similar hobbies or passions, and collab with them! The project can be literally anything—a challenge from this book, one you've seen on YouTube, or something you

two make up on your own. Some tips on finding your new friend: Search social media, join an extracurricular activity at school, or scour the comments section on my YouTube page!

CHALLENGE

#DOGWALKFORRICKY

Gather up as many dogs as you can
and see how many you can walk at
once. Start with your own if you have
one and then borrow from friends
and family. Just make sure each one
actually *likes* other dogs first!

FAMILY

My family has always been really active, and starting when I was around age seven we began an annual holiday tradition of hitting a ski resort for a week. Every year, we'd pick a different destination, and never went back to the same place twice. Not because we never enjoyed ourselves, but because we loved adventure and liked trying out new places and mountains. We traveled to Colorado, Arizona, West Virginia, and my all-time favorite, Deer Valley in Park City, Utah. The mountains up there make you feel like you're on top of the entire world. All you see around you for miles are these white-crested peaks of pure wilderness, and you really get a sense of just how huge and beautiful America is. It's pretty humbling.

Those vacations are some of my best memories growing up. I was only in second grade when we started, but my parents trusted that I was old enough not to face-plant on the bunny slopes, and it turns out that they probably could have started me out much younger. I took to skiing like a kitty to catnip—it gave me a natural high.

It's odd that I was so good at skiing right off the bat, because when I'm walking around on my plain old feet I'm normally pretty clumsy. But I remember taking one class on the kiddie hill, looking at all the other children toppling over before they even started down the four-foot slope, and being all like, "Nope, give me the mountain."

Most ski resorts use a color/shape rating system to determine the difficulty of different slopes. A green circle means easy, while double black diamonds means possible death. Tara, my dad, and I would always go for the single black diamonds, but sometimes we'd come across a double black trail that both Tara and my dad could definitely handle but I was still too young to take. I'd be able to tell that Tara wanted to follow my dad down the mountain, but she always chose to stick with me instead and take the slightly easier route. She'd use the time to help me get even better at maneuvering my skis. Since I looked up to her so much and wanted to be like her, I memorized everything she taught me and was soon tackling harder and harder trails.

Sharing the thrill of downhill skiing only reinforced my relationship with Tara. There's nothing that compares to the feeling of conquering a mountain. You know how when you're running down a hill, you're still exerting energy? When you're skiing you're just kind of sitting there and letting the snow take you along, kind of like a roller coaster on the ground. It might look and sound terrifying to some but it's utterly relaxing for me. It's the closest you'll ever get to flying without leaving the ground.

In all my years of skiing I only fell three times. They were never bad spills, although there was that one time when I fell and lost a ski and had to slide down the rest of the mountain on my butt. It was embarrassing, but also kind of fun.

My mom liked the easier slopes and would usually go off on her own, but she enjoyed the alone time. At the end of the day we'd all gather in the lodge and drink cocoa and play board games. We were super into anything that involved trivia, like Taboo, Blurt!, and Outburst. Everyone in my family has a pretty healthy competitive streak, and since we all had our individual strengths in different subjects we'd draw names from a hat to see who got paired up with whom, just to keep things interesting and different for each game.

We'd also watch holiday-themed movies on television in our lodge suite. There was always one channel that would play tons of Disney movies in a row, but my favorite holiday films are the first two entries in the *Home Alone* series. I liked to think I could be as brave as Kevin if I ever got left behind and robbers tried to invade our house!

Some years Tara would invite a friend to come along, and when she got older, her boyfriend was allowed to join us. Even in those years she'd make sure to spend a lot of time with me. I think that a lot of older siblings would choose to ditch the annoying little brother. But not her. Things weren't always perfect; she definitely teased me sometimes like any normal older sister, but never in a malicious way. Tara taught me so much about loyalty, and in a way I think she's the reason I feel so close to my viewers. She taught me that if someone looks up to you, then you should always show respect and take the person seriously.

Looking back, what I love most about those trips was that they created a tradition, and traditions are a big part of what bonds a family together. You create memories that you can share. Once you leave home, they give you something to look forward to each time you visit.

We eventually had to stop going on our ski trips because Tara got a volleyball scholarship for college, and if anything happened to her physically she could have lost the money, which would have affected her education. It didn't matter how good she was, it was still too big a risk to take.

I hope that one day we can start the tradition back up, though. Today Tara is married with a baby, and there's nothing I'd love more than to give my little niece those same kinds of memories that I was lucky enough to have growing up. It will be my turn to be the older relative teaching the younger one how to conquer mountains. I'll stay behind with her if everyone goes off to ski a harder slope. If she isn't into skiing, then we'll do something like build a snowman instead. Just like my sister did with me, I'll let her know that I will always have her back. Being there for her daughter is the least I can give my sister in return for all the sweet things she did for me growing up.

CHALLENGE

#OUTSIDEFORRICKY

Get outside! There are so many cool things to do—swim, hike, climb a tree, do handstands on the lawn, build a snowman—just show me that you love the great outdoors as much as I do. Seriously, even if it's just looking at bugs under a rock or picking a daisy. I want to see you enjoying nature!

CHALLENGE

#EMOJISFORRICKY

Act out five of your favorite emoticons. You get extra love for enlisting a friend to help you pose as the ballerina twins.

MUSIC

The first year of middle school is a huge moment in any kid's life—the big symbolic leap from childhood to preteen. I couldn't wait for it to start. Anything felt possible! No more dioramas or safety scissors for this guy. I'd spent the past six years wrapped up in an innocent childhood fog full of Game Boys and stuffed animals. The most stressful thing in my life was long division, and even that was pretty easy for me. It may be called *junior* high, but as far as I was concerned it was the big leagues and I was determined to make the most of it with my friends.

Except that suddenly my friends disappeared. Bumpus Middle School (weird name, I know) split the sixth-grade class into three groups via a random lottery system. Everyone I knew from elementary school got placed in a different group than I did. We became divided by a large hallway that ran down the middle of the school, but it might as well have been the Grand Canyon in terms of the gaping chasm that separated me from my former source of social life.

It's not like I didn't try to make new friends. The kids in my class were nice enough, but I was too busy going crazy from jealousy about all the fun stories my friends would tell me after school about what they were up to on the other side of the building. They'd all joined band and constantly raved about how cool it was, so solely in an effort to get back in with them, I decided to join band, too. It's strange how a move that was originally nothing more than a strategic grasp at keeping my social life intact ended up affecting the course of the rest of my life.

I still remember the first day I walked into the band room, with its cage-lined walls. The instruments were kept locked up, in case someone tried to walk away with a tuba and . . . what exactly? Sell it on the tuba black market? I never really understood what the school was so afraid of, but they treated those instruments like they were made of solid gold instead of finger-grubby brass.

I wasn't diving in totally blind. I'd always loved music class in elementary school. I could huff out a pretty wicked "Mary Had a Little Lamb" on the recorder, so I had a vague thought that maybe I'd play the flute or clarinet. But when I told the band teacher, Ms. Baine, that I wanted to join, she had something else in mind.

"We're low on trumpeters," she said, walking over to one of the cages, pulling a trumpet out, and handing it over. "Want to be one?"

The instrument felt good in my hands. Not too heavy, but enough weight to make it feel, I don't know, significant somehow. I put my lips to it and tried to blow.

"No, it's like this," Ms. Baine said, and pursed her lips, making a funny "pfffft" sound with them.

I copied the move and a single note burst out. I liked the sound of it, the clear tone with a little bit of bass behind it. I tried a few more times, then ran my fingers over the little taps, pushing them up and down. A series of totally random notes came out that sounded terrible together and I noticed Ms. Baine wince a little but smile encouragingly.

Over the next four months, I got better and better. My plan worked—I got to spend more time with my friends—but learning to play the trumpet was the real prize. Reading sheet music came pretty naturally to me. I could look at all those little dots and lines on the page and hear the sound each one represented in my head. Making my fingers push the right buttons was a simple matter of memorization.

Throughout middle school, all the different styles of band were rolled into one class. We'd play classical music like Beethoven's Ninth Symphony and then pep rally stuff during the school football games. Those tunes were my favorites—fight songs, the really inspirational, fun, and upbeat pieces that helped pump up the players. We'd even play things like "The Imperial March (Darth Vader's Theme)" from *Star Wars* to intimidate the other team.

Once I got to high school and joined band there, I had to automatically do both concert band and marching band. If you wanted to, you could also join jazz band, and I decided to give that a shot as well. It made for an insane schedule but I don't regret it for a second.

Our marching band uniforms were cool. I mean, I obviously wouldn't just walk around in one all the time, but I liked stomping about the football field in my tailored black suit with gold trim, topped off with a bucket hat. The thrill of looking up at the black sky, the stars totally obliterated by the field lights while our entire crew marched and played in unison, made me feel like I was part of something bigger than myself.

It sounds cheesy, but whatever. I was hardly the biggest football fan, but Hoover was definitely a high school football town, and just seeing everyone else so happy and excited made *me* happy and excited. There's nothing wrong with spreading good vibes.

I also know that the discipline was good for me. I was playing two to three times a day in my different classes. Then I'd play again after school either at a game or at marching practice, and then rehearse in my bedroom at night before bed. In all, I was either playing or practicing trumpet up to five and a half hours each day! My lips would grow numb and I probably emptied an entire lake's worth of saliva from the spit valve over the years (gross, but a necessary occupational hazard), but it was all more than worth it. Being in band helped me become the performer I am today. Even though I was just a small part of a much larger group, I could still feel the eyes of the crowd on me. It was a good way of easing me into the spotlight. I was out there on display, but I still had a protective shell of other people to help me not feel scared. As I grew more and more comfortable, I began to feel the desire to break away from the crowd and perform on my own.

CHALLENGE

#MUSICFORRICKY

Find an instrument you've never picked
up before in your life and make a video of
you playing an easy song for beginners,
maybe something like "Mary Had a Little
Lamb" or "Row, Row, Row Your Boat."
Or trying to play them, at least—no
one is perfect the first time. That's
what makes it so awesomely awful.

CHALLENGE

#ROLLFORRICKY

TP a friend's house! Just in case you're not familiar, this means tossing tons of rolls of toilet paper into trees in their front yard. And then help them clean it up later.

HEALTH

I am addicted to fitness and staying healthy. Considering all the things in the world that a person can become addicted to, I feel lucky that's the only thing I ever got hooked on. Staying in shape and eating right keeps me sane, keeps my mind focused, and relieves stress.

One big important note that I need to get out of the way up front, though: All the fitness and diet stuff that I'm going to write about here and in the rest of the book happens to be what works best for me. Everyone's body is different and everyone's health needs are different. If you're interested in getting healthier or working out to change any aspect of your body or life, it's always best to talk to a doctor or your gym teacher first so they can give advice tailored to you. Rushing into a workout program or changing your diet too fast can be hard on you, and sometimes even dangerous if you don't know what you're doing.

As for me, I plan my entire daily schedule around exercise. If I go more than two days without working out, I feel like I'm going crazy. I get all antsy and spacy and have trouble making decisions.

I like shaking up my routine every so often, but right now here's how I start my day: Mornings are for cardio, usually running or Soul Cycle. Running in the morning is the best way to burn fat and keep yourself shredded. Plus it wakes your butt up way better than coffee.

I save weight training for the evenings because you can use the food that you ate all day to help with muscle growth and strength. Doing weight training in the morning is a little harder for the basic reason that you aren't up to your optimum strength. You've been flat on your back or side or stomach for eight hours (ideally), and it helps to have your body nice and warmed up before trying to lift heavy things repeatedly.

Staying healthy achieves a whole mess of goals at once for me. It keeps me happy, and taking control of the way my body looks helps me realize that I can achieve other aspirations through the same kind of discipline. Forget the stereotype about the dumb jock—physical strength equals mental strength! Unless you're on steroids. Don't ever take steroids; they give you rage fits and veins the width of Sharpies.

A lot of people listen to music while they run, but I like to use the time to think. I live in Venice, California, so sometimes I'll do my morning run down by the beach, and other times I'll run the hiking trails in Runyon Canyon, an awesome park in L.A. Wherever I am, though, I like listening to the rhythmic thud of my footsteps and taking in the world as it flashes by me. If I let my mind go it's almost like meditating, a chance to empty my brain of any negative thoughts.

Another form of running that I do is high-intensity interval training on a treadmill, which basically means I'll slow the machine down for a minute and then sprint for another minute as fast as I can. It's super hard but a really good way to target stored fat in the body. (Plus you can be done with the whole workout in around ten minutes!) All the blood pumping through my body gets my brain revving—sometimes I use the time to come up with new video ideas.

I listen to music when I lift weights, though. I always play really happy, popular hits, stuff that gets me motivated and gets my energy up without too much of a distraction. It helps to have the encouragement, and thinking too much about something else might cause you to lose focus and drop a weight on your foot. It's better to get in the zone and concentrate on the task at hand.

Right now I have two main fitness goals—to stay lean, and to gain muscle. That might sound counterintuitive, but having muscles doesn't have to mean looking like some crazy bulging superhero. And really at the end of the day my biggest goal is to just feel happy when I look in the mirror. Which is something that doesn't always happen if I've been traveling and don't have control over what I eat.

Don't get me wrong, I love to travel, but road meals are the worst. Sure, fast food tastes delicious, but too much of it will kill you. I'm much happier when I can cook for myself or order food from any restaurant I want. I like a lot of vegetables and fruit, and all of it organic if possible. Especially now that I'm vegan! Right after I became one, I noticed an immediate difference in the way I felt. I had so much more energy and just felt cleaner somehow.

Veganism is a relatively new development in my life. I never liked meat that much to begin with, and I've always loved animals. But the real catalyst for my diet change was Trevor Moran. He and I were talking one day about trying to eat healthier, and we decided to go vegan together. He lasted exactly one meal before deciding that vegan food tasted gross, but I liked it and kept going!

I'm not the type of vegan who will jump down someone's

throat or freak out if that person is eating a steak next to me. Plus it's not something I can always 100 percent control—a restaurant might cook something in butter and I wouldn't know. I do like knowing that I'm not eating any preservatives or food dyes, though. They're nasty, and you can't digest that stuff very well.

BUT! I also think it's important to not be all hard-core militant about your diet. Cheat meals can be a really healthy part of getting fit. They give you something to look forward to and provide extra motivation to work out once you've scarfed down that pizza. (Cheeseless, for me.) Make sure to let yourself *enjoy* those cheat meals, too—you're not going to experience the full euphoria of a giant plate of French fries if you're beating yourself up the whole time for eating it. It's all about achieving a balance.

The most important thing when it comes to fitness, though, is to have fun with it. Sure, it can be tough sometimes, especially when it comes to motivating yourself, but trust me when I say that staying in shape will change your life for the better in many different ways. It boosts self-confidence and increases your chances of living longer! What better incentive do you need?

CHALLENGE

#FITNESSFORRICKY

Try a form of exercise that you've never done before. Spin class, the rowing machine, free weights, yoga—anything you want! Then take a pic or a video of you trying it right after. Lemme see you sweat!

CHALLENGE

#JENGAFORRICKY

Do the Jenga Challenge (invented
by Joey Graceffa!) with a friend. You
can see me do it with Shane Dawson
on my channel, and it's basically
regular Jenga with challenges
written on some of the blocks.

SELF-EMPOWERMENT

've always been a pretty independent person. I think I got it from my dad. He always needed his alone time when I was growing up, and I was the same way, ever since I can remember. Some days I felt like playing with kids in the neighborhood, other days I just wanted to stay inside and play video games. I know a lot of people who feel the need to be constantly surrounded by their friends, and while I definitely enjoy that at times, it's not the way I roll. Creating a balance between the two is what makes me happiest.

My independent streak really kicked into high gear when I was fifteen. I hated having to rely on anyone else for my own mobility. It didn't seem fair that I had to wait for someone to come pick me up after band or tennis practice. I was a responsible teenager who never got in trouble, and it seemed ridiculous to sit around like some first-grader when I just needed to get from point A to point B.

As my sixteenth birthday approached I could not wait to get my driver's license, and I put all of my energy into learning how to operate a car. As the date of my test got closer, I got more and more jittery. I wasn't all that great, and I noticed that whoever happened to be teaching me on a particular day would grip the door handle a little harder than normal. I was very relieved when I aced the test, and once I had my actual license, I became a much better driver. I think it was my independent streak flaring up again—after I was officially allowed to get behind the wheel, I willed myself to become great at it.

Becoming mobile changed my life dramatically. Before I got my Kia, I drove a Jeep and loved being up so high off the ground. I could do whatever I wanted and finally be in full control of my own happiness. Being the workaholic that I am, one of the first things I did was drive my butt to the mall and land myself a job in a PacSun store.

I'd always been obsessed with PacSun clothes. They're beachy with a California vibe that probably partially influenced my future move to the West Coast. I was nervous when I went in for my interview, but I dressed head to toe in PacSun and the manager noticed right off. Consider that a lesson—know everything about the company you interview for before you go in! Because it worked. I may have been a skittish mess, but they complimented me on how well their clothes fit me and I was hired on the spot.

My title was Sales Rep, and in addition to working the cash register my job involved walking the floor and going up to total strangers and asking if they needed help. All normal stuff, except for one thing—I was shy and had trouble talking to people I didn't know, much less approaching them out of the blue. The idea of a regular paycheck helped force me out of my shell. I knew if I wanted to keep my job I needed to learn how to talk to strangers. So I sucked up all my jitters and threw myself into it. Early on, encounters tended to go like this:

ME: Hello, sir, how can I help you today?
CUSTOMER: Why the heck is this shirt so darn expensive?
ME (backing away slowly with my head down): I'm sorry.

As I got more comfortable with the job I learned to stick up for myself and tell anyone who complained that I didn't set the prices. For the most part I got to help people pick out clothes that I thought would look good on them, and it turned out I had a pretty great eye for it. The happier a customer was, the easier it was to talk to that person, so I did everything I could to make the customer happy. It sounds simple, but at the time it was sort of a revelation.

Once I settled into the job, the only times things got really awkward were when we suspected someone of shoplifting. Our store didn't have its own security guard, so it was up to employees to make the call whether or not to accuse someone. I hated confrontation, it felt like I had to make a snap decision about whether or not to punch someone in the face.

It was against mall policy to accuse someone without proof, and that meant asking someone to open up his or her bag, using a very nice and neutral tone of voice. But let's face it. Asking people in your store to open their bag so you can check the contents basically *is* accusing them of shoplifting.

We were taught to keep an eye on anyone who wore a big backpack into the store, and always made sure to count the number of items that went in and out of a dressing room. I was lucky, I never had a scary encounter. The few times that I knew people had stolen something and approached them, they immediately apologized and offered to pay for it. What could I do? Tell them, "No, you can't have it now because you tried to steal it?" I wasn't going to turn down a sale. So I'd ring the person up and we'd avoid eye contact and that was that. So awkward.

Aside from those few occasions, having my license and my

own source of income changed me in a big way. I was doing something for myself that would propel me further in life. A lot of people complain about having a job, but if you use it as a learning experience like I did, then it's awesome. I also lucked out because I loved all of my coworkers, and they made working there a blast. Folding and selling clothes might not sound like much fun, but it truly was for me because I *made* it fun by having a positive attitude about it. I guess Mary Poppins was right about her sugar theory.

CHALLENGE

#LAUNDRYFORRICKY

Knowing how to fold clothes is a very important life skill. Surprise your parent/sibling/roommate by doing their laundry, folding it all in nice neat stacks, and leaving it on their bed. Take a selfie with the clothes, and make sure to separate whites from darks!

CHALLENGE

#LYRICSFORRICKY

Make up your own lyrics to one of my
songs or your favorite song of all time.

RANDOM

'm twenty-four years old, and I love Pokémon. I'm not afraid to admit it—there's no shame in that game. In fact, the actual games are pretty hard! And besides, it's not like I'm an adult and still drooling over Barney or Teletubbies.

It all started with Pokémon Red and Blue for Game Boy. I was so obsessed. The basic premise is you get sent out into the world on your own to collect critters and do battle, so it's this awesome combination of whimsical imaginary animals and fierce fights. Plus no one ever dies if they lose, they just faint. It's like training wheels for real life.

I was also into Yu-Gi-Oh!, and would even enter official tournaments where I'd kick butt with my card-fighting techniques. But it wasn't the same as my love for Pokémon.

There are more than seven hundred different kinds (gotta catch 'em all!), but my absolute favorite is Ampharos. He looks like a yellow dinosaur with a white belly and flippers for arms, and what makes him special is this: Pokémon are usually divided into two categories: uber cute or awesome fighter. Ampharos is a rare combo of both. Other faves include Bulbasaur (a frog thing with a plant bulb on his back), Piplup (basically a penguin, and I live for penguins), Sceptile (a reptile with a tail that looks like palm fronds), and Sylveon (My Little Pony on acid).

Pretty much everyone I knew growing up was into

Pokémon, but as soon as I hit middle school it became very uncool to still like them. We were graduating into our teenage years and most people were desperate to leave their childhood behind and prepare for everything puberty had to offer. It's a bridge time in anyone's life, but I didn't see why I needed to give up something I loved so much in order to cross it. To put it in Pokémon terms, it was an unfair trade. You were considered a loser and super lame if you still held on to any shred of your childhood, even though I'll bet you anything that a ton of other kids were still secretly playing, too. I had to go underground, but I was still eventually caught. I have no idea how the kid found out—maybe it was just a lucky guess—but this one guy told our whole gym class that I still played Pokémon and everyone laughed and made fun of me. I remember this one girl sneering and saying, "Everyone stopped liking that years ago, what's wrong with you?"

Nothing! It honestly sounds so stupid to explain this because I know it's not even a big deal now. Like, who cares? But at the time it was *such* a huge deal and I was so embarrassed and sad.

I know lots of people my age now who are also still obsessed with Pokémon. In fact, it's considered kind of cool, at least in my circle of friends. I have a ton of toys and stuffed animals, as anyone who watched my videos when I lived with Kian and Jc in Hollywood knows. I always filmed in front of a huge wall of my collection of hundreds of Pokémon. I haven't set them up in my new place yet, but I plan to get a custom-made shelf built for them, so I can display them like art. Especially since I have so many new ones now! I recently got a chance to go to the flagship Pokémon store in Japan, where you can buy a lot of

Pokémon stuff that isn't available anywhere else in the world. I was like a kid in a candy store, if the candy were a bunch of weird-looking stuffed animals. This is kind of embarrassing, but I filled up four huge bags with new toys and had to buy a whole extra suitcase to fly home with in order to fit them all in!

I think it's really important to hold on to things you loved from childhood. Everyone always talks about the importance of listening to your inner child, but I think you should do more than just listen to it. Open up your toy box and dust off some old friends! The best way to grow old is to stay young at heart.

CHALLENGE

#TOYSFORRICKY

I want to meet your favorite toy!
Take a picture of it or make a quick
video and tell me about the cool
imaginary adventures you used
to have together. (Or still do!)

CHAPTER 2

BUMMED OUT

CHALLENGE

#SOURFACEFORRICKY

Get as many different sour candy products as you can find and try to eat as many of them in a row as possible.

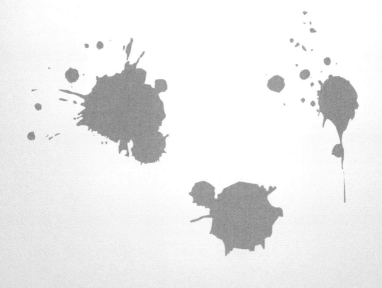

HEALTH

No matter how good you are at something, there's always a possibility that you will fail if you're only given one chance to prove your worth. It doesn't matter if you're trying out for a school play, a YouTube collab, or band—putting yourself out there can cause even the most confident people to feel like their stomach is churning out ten thousand rabid butterflies. No wonder people choke.

For me, sports auditions were the most nerve-racking. Athletics were a MAJOR deal at Hoover High. MTV even filmed a couple of seasons of a reality show called *Two-A-Days* about our football team and some of its players, sort of a true version of *Friday Night Lights*. (Behind the scenes, things were just as dramatic—it was later revealed that our school's coach was living a double life with two wives!)

I spent most of my life playing tennis with my mom and dad. I started to get really into it in junior high, and played in local competitions outside of school. But when it came time to actually try out for my school's team in eighth grade, I psyched myself out and didn't make it. Instead of getting depressed, I became all the more determined to make the ninth-grade team. So I spent the entire next year practicing my butt off. I'd play any chance I could get and by the time freshman year tryouts came around I was positive I'd land a spot.

Like I said, the problem with tryouts is that you only have

the one chance to prove your worth. You could be the best around, but if you slip up and make a mistake, which even the pros do, a coach can think that's all you're good for. With tennis it was especially difficult—if you're auditioning for a musical you have the director's full attention, but with my tennis tryout there were eight different games happening on eight different courts, in addition to other people doing drills. There was so much happening at once, and the coach would walk up and down the length of the courts, watching only one match at a time. So of course whenever I'd show off a particularly awesome backhand swing he'd be off looking at someone else, and only ever glanced over at me when I'd fault on a serve. I think subconsciously I could feel his eyes suddenly swing my way and I'd let my fear of failure get the best of me.

I couldn't figure out how he managed to see ONLY my mistakes, though. Not to sound arrogant, but I knew I was good. My friends knew I was good. My family did too. In fact, everyone seemed to know it except the one person who mattered most. So when I didn't make the team everyone was sort of shocked, especially my friend Mason.

Mason and I had met in band and become really close. He has dark hair, is just as tall as I am, and we had *everything* in common—he also played trumpet, we were both really into tennis, and we'd have sleepovers all of the time where we'd watch movies and play video games.

When he landed a spot on the team I went to all the school matches to watch him play, because I'm not a petty person. I was secretly sad, though. It sucked to watch him out there on the court, having fun. His being on the team was suddenly the *only* thing we didn't have in common.

I refused to let not getting on the team lessen my resolve, though. I practiced harder than ever, determined to make the high school team. Mason helped me a lot, and that whole year whenever we had a sleepover we'd wake up early in the morning and go practice at one of the many, many tennis courts that for some reason are all over Hoover. We had a healthy rivalry in most things we did together, but I'm not too proud to admit that he was better than me at tennis. It was the drive to catch up to him that finally got me on the team. He made me want to get even better, and it worked—I made varsity the next year!

CHALLENGE

#SPORTSFORRICKY

If you've never done it, play my favorite game, tennis! If you've already played tennis even once in your life, choose a different

sport you've never attempted
and give it a go. It's totally okay
if you're terrible at it. Or maybe
you'll discover a hidden talent!

CHALLENGE

#SHIPFORRICKY

Ship two characters from your
favorite movie, book, or TV show
and make a video explaining why
they're perfect for each other.

MUSIC

For someone who was as big a band geek as I was, it's no shocker that I was into all different kinds of music growing up. Because of my age, Britney Spears has always been playing somewhere in the background pretty much my whole life. In fact, I love all the big pop diva queens like Katy Perry and Demi Lovato. But there's also a side of me that really loves alternative punk bands like All Time Low, Blink-182, and All-American Rejects.

In fact, I loved All-American Rejects so much that I did my first solo music video ever to them. All of the ones I'd filmed with Shelby were fun and sort of silly, but I decided to take this one seriously. The piece they did for "Move Along" is made up of a ton of fast-cut edits, with the lead singer standing still but changing outfits and locations about a million different times. It's almost like stop-motion animation, and it was a form of editing that I'd been playing around with a lot in my free time anyway. So I studied it really hard and spent over a week creating my own version and lip-syncing along. That was probably the first time that my passion for making videos hit super hard. I'd always enjoyed it, but working on that video didn't *feel* like work. It was playtime for me.

It had been about a year since I'd stopped doing videos with Shelby. I was proud of how "Move Along" turned out and I uploaded it to our old PICKLEandBANANA YouTube channel. We only had about forty subscribers, and they were pretty much my family members and people I knew from band. I wanted other people to see my new creation, so I sent out mass Facebook messages with links to the video, and posted it on my own Facebook page as well. You know, Marketing 101.

That minimal bit of effort backfired, majorly.

I can't even put into words how hard I was bullied and harassed about that first attempt at creative expression. Well, okay, I'll try. Imagine busting your butt for days on end, working on a labor of love that filled you with a sense of purpose and hope and curiosity for the future. Now imagine showing the final product to people and being flat-out laughed at. People trashed that video like a moldy sandwich, and I was humiliated.

The thing was, I still thought it was good. I couldn't understand what they saw in it that I didn't. It was just a video, clearly meant to be lighthearted and fun, and I'd put a lot of time and effort into it. As the online taunting progressed, it started to bleed out into real life. Students at my school would convince teachers to screen it in class on big projectors, under the guise of its having something to do with whatever they were studying. The teacher would hit play, unaware that the entire class was mocking it. Kids made fun of me in the hallway, singing the song and imitating my moves. I was the talk of the entire school for weeks. I realize this might sound overdramatic, and I'm not one to look for pity, but the experience was miserable. I could not escape the ridicule and harassment surrounding the video and it went on for weeks on end.

During this time I tried to keep my head held high but I felt like I was dying inside. I was not just ready to delete the video, I wanted to delete my entire channel.

I decided to go and talk to Ms. Pierce, my favorite teacher.

She taught history and coincidentally happened to keep moving up a grade every year, so I always had class with her. She listened patiently while I explained what had been happening, but refused to let me wallow in my misery. She told me that I had a knack for making videos, and that I needed to stick with it no matter what the student body reaction was. It wasn't any sort of big speech, and she probably didn't realize it at the time, but she singlehandedly had one of the most positive impacts ever on my life. She was there during a time I needed someone the most, and hearing some positivity from her meant so much. I still think about it all of the time. I hope she knows how amazing she is.

"Some people don't understand creativity," she told me. "But you do. You clearly have it."

I felt a little better after I left her classroom, but it was really Shelby who helped me fully pull through. As always, she was my faithful cheerleader and supporter.

"It doesn't matter what people say," she said. "This could be a big thing for you one day."

It was near impossible to imagine that being true at the time, considering the reaction I'd gotten. It was like studying to be a dentist and accidentally getting your hands chopped off and everyone's like, "No problem! You can still fulfill your dream of scraping plaque off strangers' teeth!" Okay, not exactly the same, but that's what it felt like.

I stuck it out, though. I kept the video up, ate all the abuse, and in the end Shelby was right. Eventually some other poor kid did something that caused the herd to focus its nastiness elsewhere. I was blissfully forgotten and continued making my videos in peace. It took a while for me to get up the guts to promote something I'd made as much as I did that first time, though. I'd been scarred badly, but I kept on going.

The takeaway here is pretty obvious—don't listen to haters. But I think the more important thing to realize is that if you are being attacked or bullied, it helps a lot to talk to someone about it. It can be a parent, a friend, a teacher, a sibling, really anyone in your life whom you trust. The important thing is to not keep those bad feelings to yourself. They will fester like an ingrown hair and make you doubt your abilities. Worse, they could keep you from doing the things in life you love. There's that old saying, "If at first you don't succeed, try, try again," but I think that advice should go a step further when it comes to creativity and imagination. If you've managed to actually make something yourself and people don't like it, the fact that you even took that first step to create is success in and of itself. That's not to say it isn't important to practice and hone your craft. And also be sure you don't fall into the trap of mixing up constructive criticism with ridicule—sometimes there are actually important things you can learn from someone's not-exactly-positive reaction. But I think the difference between the two is usually pretty clear.

In the end, I did take the video down, but for a much more lame reason—copyright issues. But it was another important lesson: Always make sure that what you're posting on YouTube is legal. Back then it was a lot harder to figure out the rules, but now YouTube has a whole library where you can check specific songs to see what their copyright details are and find out whether you can use the song. Most are actually fine now, because YouTube will place ads on the video to pay the song owner, but you should always check first before posting anything!

CHALLENGE

#REMAKEFORRICKY

I officially give you permission to use any of my songs! Make a music video, either singing or lip-syncing, to any one you want, using your own creative vision!

CHALLENGE

#POOLFORRICKY

Jump into a public pool with
all of your clothes on.

FAMILY

f I have anyone to thank for my creative genes, it's my aunt Vickie. She was my dad's sister, and I saw her more often than any other members of our extended family (aside from my grandparents) simply because she lived in Atlanta, so it was pretty easy for her to come and visit us. My mom has siblings, too, but they lived on the other side of the country.

Aunt Vickie loved to change up her look on a regular basis, and always rocked some new haircut every time I saw her. One month her short hair would be brown, and the next, bleached blond. She had a fantastic sense of style, and I always looked forward to seeing what she'd be wearing when she showed up. Sometimes everything was bright and colorful, and one time she arrived at the house dressed like a full-on cowgirl! She'd never just wear jeans and a shirt. She was flamboyant, funny, and fierce. I adored her.

She ran a picture-framing business and did her own photography and graphic design on the side, so she was the first person I knew who made a living by doing something artistic. She was an incredible painter and drawer, and we have tons of her artwork hanging in our house. She didn't have any kids of her own, so she always made sure to spend as much time with Tara and me as possible.

I had a special bond with Aunt Vickie, and she was around for every birthday, graduation, and holiday. My earliest memories of her are of her coming over for Christmas and decorating cookies with me. We'd come up with fantastic colorful designs that didn't adhere to any kind of specific holiday rules. I'd pile on seven different colors of icing in swirls and patterns, and the crazier I got with my creations the more she loved them. I lived for making her happy and proud of me, and I always felt like she understood me on a much different level than most people in my life.

On Easter Sunday of my junior year in high school, she came over for our annual feast. We had always dyed eggs together, but for whatever reason—teenage hormones, a desire to seem more grown-up—I decided I didn't want to that year. She seemed a little disappointed but quickly brushed it off.

Not dyeing those eggs with her is one of the biggest regrets of my life.

One month later, she was diagnosed with soft tissue sarcoma, a type of cancer that forms tumors in muscle and bone. It came out of nowhere, and we were told there was nothing the doctors could do. The cancer had advanced too far for chemotherapy. I was in shock when we drove to Atlanta to see her, and even more so when I laid eyes on her. Just four weeks earlier she had been her normal, healthy, full-of-energy self. What I saw when we arrived was a pale, scarily skinny woman with sunken eyes. But her attitude was the same. She knew what was happening to her and accepted it. She reassured us instead of the other way around. She tried to make us laugh and told jokes and acted like nothing was different, even as we moved her into hospice care. Despite her fading looks, she seemed so full of life that I couldn't grasp she was actually dying.

Her doctors warned us that the end would come fast, and

my parents told me before one particular visit that it would probably be the last. Instead of long tearful good-byes, we pretended nothing was different, because we knew that was how she would want it. There were a million things I wanted to say to her that I felt I couldn't, but the beautiful thing about our relationship is that I didn't really need to. She knew how I felt about her, and I felt all that love returned when I looked into her eyes as I said good-bye. A few weeks later she passed away. The last words she ever said to me were "I'm so proud of you," and she smiled the same bright smile I'd known all my life.

I was devastated. It was my first experience with death, and I had no idea what to do with all the emotions I had. In retrospect, I think I went through all the normal stages of grief, from denial to acceptance, but each step felt like I was floating through a fog instead of truly experiencing the feelings for what they needed to be.

I didn't fully feel her loss until I started to get serious about my YouTube channel around six months after she died. No one in my family quite understood what it was all about, but I knew that she would have. She was always so attuned to the world as it changed around her, and I know that she would have embraced the new digital era with the same enthusiasm and curiosity that she did everything else. When people made fun of my videos I swear I could hear her far away in the background, cheering me on and giving me the support I needed to continue.

When loved ones die they may be gone in body, but they never really leave you. They live on in your memories, and the closer you were to them, the more you can feel them supporting you when you need advice or comfort. Not in a creepy ghost way, but more like a guardian angel looking over you, with a little voice in the back of your head that tells you to keep going when your confidence is dwindling, or you're hurt or sad. Sometimes it's something as simple as the memory of Aunt Vickie's laugh that can get me on my feet again if I'm down. This made me realize that even the smallest things you do in your life can have the power to change or help others. I know I'm not the only person in this world who was affected by Aunt Vickie's incredible spirit. Because of her, I try to give some of those good vibes back to others in my YouTube videos.

The other big thing I learned from Aunt Vickie's death is to cherish every second of every moment that you get with someone you love. That last Easter we had together still haunts me. If only I hadn't been so wrapped up in myself I would have had one more awesome memory of us hanging out together. The fact is, no one is ever too old to dye Easter eggs.

CHALLENGE

#CRAFTSFORRICKY

Spend quality time with a loved
one creating an arts and crafts
project together. Introduce whoever
your own personal Aunt Vickie is
and show the finished piece!

CHALLENGE

#STRANGERLANGUAGEFORRICKY

Approach a stranger and start
speaking to him or her in a
totally made-up language.

SELF-EMPOWERMENT

By the time I turned five, it was pretty clear to my parents that when I called my sister "Tawa" instead of Tara, it was the result of a speech impediment and not an attempt to hold on to my youth by speaking baby talk. I was basically Elmer Fudd with a full head of hair.

The condition is called rhotacism (try saying that with a speech impediment). I won't bore you with all of the physiological reasons behind it, but suffice it to say other kids my age weren't too nice about its effect on my voice. My biggest memory from kindergarten isn't learning how to read, it's the other children sneering, "Why do you talk like that?" before walking away and building castles out of wooden blocks without me.

It took most of elementary school to train my tongue to find the right spot in my mouth to form R sounds. Every other day I'd get called out of class to go to speech therapy, where I'd be given a list of about fifty words to repeat over and over. I had to memorize the muscle movement in my tongue that for whatever reason didn't come naturally to my mouth. I'd make my way through workbooks of increasing difficulty, and spend time on my own at home practicing words like "repeater," "radar," and "reader."

The main thing that sucked about the process was my embarrassment over even having to go to speech therapy. I lied about where I was going when I got called out of a normal class, often elaborately. Why anyone believed that I got to skip out on math because I'd been asked by the principal to build a special float for a parade is beyond me. Students probably knew I was making the whole thing up, especially since neither the float nor a parade ever materialized. I don't want to promote lying, but look, like most kids, I just wanted to fit in. I was beyond embarrassed about it so I just made up stories as an easy way out of having to explain anything. There was nothing worse than being called on to answer a question in class. The main subjects you learn in school are literally called "the Three Rs." Or as I knew them, "the Three Ws."

By sixth grade, I'd worked long and hard enough to get rid of the problem. When I spoke, I knew where my tongue was supposed to land in order to make the correct sounds. I finally talked like a normal person! My classmates basically forgot that I'd ever had a problem speaking. But then disaster struck—my braces.

My teeth had always been a little off. Nothing super rugged or anything, but my top row didn't align with the bottom at all, and as I grew older, the divide grew bigger. So instead of just straightening my teeth out, the braces also shifted the shape of my jaw line. An unintentional side effect was that my tongue now slipped off my top teeth, creating what seemed like a lisp, but technically wasn't a normal, natural one. My braces warped my teeth, so after years and years of fixing one speech problem, I was suddenly slapped with another, and I had to start a whole new course of speech therapy! But I was never able to quite shake this one. These days it's nowhere near as bad as it used to be, but obviously anyone who has seen one of my videos knows it's there. In the early days of my YouTube channel, I got a lot of nasty comments about it, but years of hearing taunts in person had pretty much desensitized me to anything that some loser who is too scared to even show his real name has to say about the way I talk. Today, it's still the main subject of any kind of hate comments I get on my videos. They don't affect me at all, though. I don't know if it's because I'm just so used to them by now, but more likely it's because I've learned to accept that part of myself.

I've made peace with my voice. It makes me unique. The way I talk is part of who I am, and learning to love yourself is one of the most important things to do if you want to live a healthy, happy, and productive life. My voice hasn't stopped me from shooting videos, singing, or making friends.

I've got too much that I want to accomplish to let something as basic as a speech issue affect my goals. Everyone has physical traits that they can't change, and everyone has something about themselves that they are self-conscious about. I can guarantee you that even the most seemingly perfect people you know have something that they hate about themselves. Insecurity is a natural part of life, as normal as feeling happy or sad. It sucks that we live in a culture designed to breed more physical anxiety than past generations ever had to deal with, and while I think that social media definitely plays a huge part in that, I think it can also be a major force for good. Look at campaigns like NOH8 or It Gets Better—they take the same platforms that can cause people to feel bad about themselves and turn them into safe spaces that celebrate individuality.

If there's even just one kid out there who has a speech issue similar to mine and is being bullied because of it, I hope that he'll see one of my videos and realize he can move far beyond letting idiots get to him. The fact that I have a singing career should show people that a speech impediment doesn't have to get in the way of their dreams. It's not how it sounds that's important when you say something, it's the words that come out of your mouth that matter.

CHALLENGE

#CONFIDENTFORRICKY

Tell a story about something you
used to be insecure about and how
you managed to overcome those
feelings and be more confident.

CHALLENGE

#SPINTHEBOTTLEFORRICKY

Play spin the bottle, but instead of
kissing people, set up a circle of
the nastiest foods you can find.

SOCIAL

I n ninth grade, our high school guidance counselors told us we needed to go ahead and choose what we wanted our major to be in college. Which is just insane. You might *think* you know what you want to do with the rest of your life at age fourteen, but it usually changes, and often on a daily basis.

When it finally came time for me to actually apply, I was just getting into YouTube so it hadn't occurred to me at all that it could be a career. So I took the easy way out and decided to follow in my father's footsteps and study pharmacy. Auburn University, which is about two hours southeast of Hoover, offered it as a major. I was good at math and science, which I knew would help, but even better, a whole bunch of my friends ended up getting into the same school as well. Including Mason! I figured I'd have a built-in support system.

Mason and I decided to be roommates, but neither of us had any desire to live in a dorm. Fortunately, the school offered campus apartments that were set up more like town houses, and we were lucky enough to be able to afford one. (I really, really didn't want to have to share a bathroom with an entire floor of other dudes. Gross!)

You know how everyone says that college is the time when you make the friends you will have for life? Not so much in my case. I joined band because that's what I knew and loved, and I went to classes and got good grades, but I didn't have much of a social life. Scratch that, I had ZERO social life.

College marching band wasn't the same as high school. For one thing, it was way bigger, which made it harder to connect and bond with people. I got invited to a few parties, but since I had never gone to any in high school, I couldn't imagine how I was supposed to act at a college rager. Keg stand? Funneling? They sounded like advanced yoga poses to me. There were also always parties happening around our apartment complex, and Mason would try to get me to go out with him, but I much preferred staying in, making videos and talking with my YouTube friends. I just didn't like being around drunken strangers— they were loud and obnoxious and every time I saw someone puking on the quad it freaked me out.

It didn't take long for me to drift away from my high school friends who also attended Auburn. They quickly formed new social circles and started to discover themselves. All normal stuff, and while it made me a little sad I was also happy for them because whenever I did see them around campus they looked like they were having so much fun. I didn't hold any sort of grudge against them for moving on, mainly because I knew I was the one holding myself back.

There was one friendship I did regret losing, though. Around the middle of the year, Mason and his girlfriend got more and more serious. As I kept declining his invitations to hang out with them, he started to spend more and more time at her apartment. On the one hand: Score! I now had the place to myself most of the time. But on the other, I was totally alone. Mason and I started to drift apart even more, especially after he quit band after our freshman year. After that, I rarely saw him at all.

I thought maybe I could find friends at the gym since I was still making sure to work out a lot, but I quickly realized that there was a chain gym located much closer to my apartment than the one on campus, where I would have actually met other students. So that eliminated another possibility for meeting other college kids.

I'm not that great when it comes to decorating, and our apartment always looked pretty sparse. I didn't hang anything on the walls, so when Mason decided to unofficially permanently move in with his girlfriend, the place felt even more barren. He was still paying rent, but I suddenly had the entire town house to myself 24/7. I'd sit alone in the living room, listening to the sound of music thumping through the walls next door, and feel, well, not lonely exactly. It was more that I knew emphatically that something was missing. I wasn't happy, and it wasn't just my lack of friends. It was about a lack of interest in life itself, which is infinitely more depressing. It's not like I was suicidal or anything, I just knew I had accidentally entered onto a path that wasn't meant for me. I was doing fine in my pharmacy classes, but they bored me to tears. The idea that I might have to spend the rest of my life working behind a counter at a drugstore, counting out heart medicine pills while customers screamed at me about their health insurance issues from the other side of the counter, was totally unacceptable. And forget trying to become close to anyone within that major—everyone was so dedicated to studying that none of them seemed to be looking for new friends either. I needed to make a change.

So I started to put a plan into action. I changed my major to film, hoping that I'd meet more people who liked the same sorts of things I did. That didn't exactly work out either, though. The program was all about technical stuff that I already knew how to do. I realized my mistake within the first week—I wanted to be in front of the camera, not behind it. Even though it seemed almost immediately like another misstep, the important thing was that I took action. I recognized that I was sad and instead of wallowing around and eating doughnuts and closing all the blinds I made a conscious decision to change the things that were bumming me out. And even though I still didn't make any new friends, it did start me off on the right course to find some. Without being a film major, I never would have gotten my film internship, which was what finally got me to Los Angeles. If you feel like you've got no friends, change things up! Put yourself out there by joining extracurricular activities. If you hate your school, look for other places in your town that will expose you to new people, such as a community theater. The most important thing to realize, though, is that if that doesn't work, all you have to do is try something else. Life paths are rarely a straight line, and you just have to keep moving. You never know where you'll pick up a friend along the way.

I just realized that's essentially the plot of *The Wizard of Oz*, but trust me, it's true.

CHALLENGE

#ACTINGFORRICKY

Re-create your favorite moment from your favorite film! But if you go with that "I'm the king of the world" scene from *Titanic*, DON'T do it on an actual boat. Play safe, people!

CHALLENGE

#MASSAGEFORRICKY

**Offer to give strangers a
free back massage.**

RANDOM

This next story is more mildly pathetic than sad, but it was a big part of my formative years. You know how everyone has their own way of reacting to stressful situations? Some people bite their fingernails; others fidget a lot, tug nervously at their hair, or shuffle their feet, which can look kind of endearing and cute. But my method was definitely just gross. For years, I used to spontaneously puke any time I was nervous or had anxiety about anything.

It started on the first day of junior high. As soon as my mom pulled up in front of the school and I saw all these teenagers hanging out in front of the four giant white columns that framed the stern brick building, I panicked and felt the first waves of nausea hit me. There were so many people, all of them much older and infinitely cooler than me. *Deep breaths*, I told myself.

I managed to keep it together until first period. I slid into my assigned seat next to a girl named Jasmine whom I vaguely knew from elementary school. I felt relieved to see a somewhat familiar face, since all my friends had been placed in the other class. I gave her a wobbly grin as we stood up to say the Pledge of Allegiance. She ignored me, but not for long.

I got as far as "to the flag" before I spontaneously erupted my breakfast all over Jasmine and her obviously brand-new, first-day-of-school outfit. My own, as well, but I didn't care so much about that. I ran from the room to the sounds of kids screaming, laughing, and making generally grossed-out noises. I tried to contain all the bile and bits of pancake dribbling off my body but left an incriminating trail down the hallway behind me, my very first walk of shame. I made it to the bathroom, locked myself in a stall, and emptied the rest of my stomach. Jasmine, if you're reading this, I'm so sorry for ruining your first day of middle school.

Fortunately, this one kid named David, whom I later became really good friends with, came to check on me in the bathroom and walked me back to class. I barely knew him at that point, and it meant a lot. Thank you for rescuing me, David!

The next year, I woke up on the first day of school filled with dread and a feeling like there was a tiny boxing match going on in my stomach. I made sure not to eat breakfast so that there would be nothing for me to puke once I got to campus, but I stupidly took a big drink from the water fountain as I entered the school. The liquid soon spouted right back up, but I made it to the bathroom in time. The next year, I made sure to not even drink water, but still spewed the previous night's dinner (spaghetti, as I was reminded) right before first period. School was literally making me gag.

I hoped this would all be over by the time I reached high school. I had three years of middle school behind me to prepare myself for the fear of facing a new year. Nope. I didn't even make it past the front door of Hoover High, and instead christened the building by upchucking all over the flagpole. Luckily, no one was around from the day I puked on Jasmine, so I was able to tell the kids who saw me do it that I had a stomach bug.

Which made them avoid me anyway, but at least it was because they thought I was contagious, and not a loser who couldn't handle stress.

This continued for about another year and a half. Any time I had to do something important, like audition for band or tennis, I'd feel that old familiar seasick wave and make it to the bathroom in time to spew. It was my routine when it came to any sort of challenge. I had to puke it out before I'd duke it out.

I can't really remember the last time it happened, but I know it stopped around the middle of high school. By that point I'd made a bunch of friends, I had band, I was on the tennis team. Which makes me think that all of that vomiting amounted to nothing more than an extreme physical reaction to a fear of being alone and not accepted. Which are totally normal things to feel, especially during big moments like the first day of school or an audition. For some reason my body took it into overdrive, and while that wasn't really in my control, what *was* in my control was steeling my nerves and putting myself out there in order to make those feelings of inadequacy go away.

To this day I still feel a little queasy any time I'm about to do something scary like go onstage or begin an important business meeting. But I just take a few deep breaths and remind myself of how far I've come. And then I'll call or text Shelby if neither of those works. If you don't have a Shelby in your life, here are some things to think about to help you get over being scared about the first day of school. (I'm just using that as an example since it caused the most anxiety in me—this technique can apply to just about anything, such as hanging out with a new group of people.) Chances are, everyone else in the room is probably just as scared as you are. Even the person who seems the bravest is harboring a little bit of uncertainty deep inside. That's human nature. You are not alone in your feelings. Take a look around and remember that.

When it comes to scary moments like an audition for the school play or band, think of it this way: Nobody wants you to fail. The director might seem scary, but he or she just wants you to do your best. You're in the situation together. And hey, even if you projectile vomit into the audience (like Aubrey did in *Pitch Perfect*) at least you've made a memorable impression.

CHALLENGE

#PUKEPRANKFORRICKY

Get some fake rubber vomit, leave it
somewhere surprising, and film the
reaction! Can't find fake vomit? Make
your own with stuff from the kitchen, but
be sure to leave it on an easily cleanable
surface. Vomit too nasty for you? Get
creative and invent your own gross prank!

CHAPTER 3

AMBITION

CHALLENGE

#COSTUMESFORRICKY

Dress up in an elaborate Halloween costume and go grocery shopping as if everything is normal. Make sure the date isn't within two months of October 31.

FAMILY

Remember how I said I had no friends back in college? That isn't exactly true. I'd been friends online with my future O2L members Jc, Kian, Connor, Trevor, and Sam, as well as other YouTubers like Jack Baran, Andrew Lowe, and Andrea Russett for months before I ever met any of them in person. We all liked each other's videos, subscribed to each other's channels, and chatted via Skype and IM all the time, and even though we weren't hanging out in person I still felt that same chemistry you get from being in close proximity, those invisible threads that link you to someone.

So I was super pumped to finally meet them all in person at VidCon during my sophomore year of college. The future O2L boys and I all planned to share one tiny hotel room! It was pretty cool that people who had physically never been in the same room together could click as fast as we did. You could almost hear our future snapping into place when we all met up for the first time. We spent the entire conference wandering around, freaking out over our favorite YouTube stars and asking to take selfies with them.

I think our first big bonding moment happened at VidCon's annual District Lines party—which we weren't invited to. District Lines is this huge YouTuber merchandising company, and every year they throw this fancy party that only the biggest YouTubers and their friends and managers are welcome to attend. So of course we tried to get in, strutting up to the front door and pretending we'd lost our invites. The bouncers were not having it, and we got, well, bounced.

Getting turned away from any party is always a huge bummer, but we'd been having such a good time so far that we refused to let getting rejected bring us down. We were determined to get into that party, one way or another. So we scoped out the perimeter and realized that there was a back entrance through the kitchen.

Here's the only real trick you need to know in order to sneak into an event. Act like you belong. We sauntered right through the kitchen like we owned the place and before we knew it we were inside. (Side note: I don't think there's any way this could happen nowadays. Security is MUCH tighter!)

The party was everything we could have hoped for. It was filled with YouTube megastars. I was constantly like, "OMG, there's Jenna Marbles! There's Grace Helbig!" And then I'd run over to them and snap selfies. I'm sure they were thinking, *Who is this annoying kid?* Funny thing is, everyone I acted like a total fanboy over and asked for pictures of is now a good friend! It's kind of embarrassing to remember how I acted when I first met them.

My friends and I stalked the room that night, trying to chat up as many people as we could, having no idea that the following year *we'd* be the ones on the special guest list!

The conference was so much fun that we didn't want it to end. Sam and Kian lived in San Clemente, which is just a little over an hour away from L.A., and we all ended up staying at Sam's house for an entire week. And that's where Our2ndLife began.

I'm assuming that most of you reading this know what O2L is, but just in case you don't, it was a collab channel that we all formed together, a sort of super collective. Each of us was responsible for posting a video on a different day of the week (mine was Tuesday), and since we each individually had decent followings, once we combined forces O2L became a ridiculously huge success almost overnight.

Everything happened very fast with O2L, especially after I moved to L.A. (that story's coming up). There were tours, photo shoots, red carpet appearances—it was all almost too much to absorb. But it was the most fun I think I've ever had in my life. More important, I realized that I'd not only created a collab channel with these guys, I'd created a second family. Even though O2L is done now, these guys are my brothers for life.

I have a lot of viewers who send messages to me about not getting along with their families, or worse, being totally estranged from them. Coming from a place of such security myself, it's difficult for me to even fathom what that must feel like. But it makes my heart ache to imagine. What's important to remember is that family comes from where you decide to make one. Just because you're related to a person through blood, that doesn't automatically make them family. Okay, well, *technically* it does, but what I'm saying is that many people have found their true families outside the ones they grew up with. Family means unconditional love, no matter what. If you're not getting that from people who raised you, look for it somewhere else and create your own.

On a more upbeat note, even if you already have an awesome family, you can still have a whole separate one with your friends! I would do anything for people in my life like Shelby and Connor, just like I would do anything for Tara or my parents. My love for all of them comes with no strings attached, and I know they feel the same way. That's what having a real family is all about.

CHALLENGE

#THROWBACKFORRICKY

Post a throwback picture of you and
one of your closest friends from
around the time you first met.

CHALLENGE

#BALLOONSFORRICKY

Get a bunch of friends together and blow
up hundreds and hundreds of balloons
inside a room. Get them at least one foot
deep so you have a personal ball pit!

SELF-EMPOWERMENT

Whenever I was in my college apartment, I'd have anywhere from two to six different chat windows open, carrying on different conversations with the O2L boys and other YouTuber friends.

Kian was just getting started making music videos, so I'd give him tutorials on how to edit. More often than not, though, we'd all just hang out over video calls. I'd do my homework while they did their own thing in their house. We didn't even need to be having a conversation; it just felt nice having someone in the room with me. Well, someone's voice and image with me. Sometimes we'd even have iChat sleepovers! We'd stay up super late talking and then all leave our computers on when we went to bed.

After we had all finally met in person at VidCon and decided to form O2L, I knew it was time to make a real change. College was making me miserable, and I knew in my heart that YouTube was my future. Switching to film hadn't really changed much for me. If anything, it was making things worse. It was like I was close to doing what I wanted, but not quite there. I wanted to be in *front* of the camera, not just doing lighting and editing and camera work. I was already doing all of that stuff on my own.

I started to put my secret plan into action. I knew I wanted to drop out of school and move to L.A., but I also knew there was no way my parents would go for that. I needed to figure out a way to get out there, so I asked my dad if he could help me research internships.

"All the serious film stuff is in L.A.," I told him. "The only way I can get real experience is if I'm out there." He agreed, and helped me apply for a few different internships, but I only heard back from one production company, which for privacy's sake I'm going to call West Coast Productions. WCP was run by a guy named Greg (again, fake name), and I talked to him on the phone a few times about the job before my dad agreed to sublease a small one-bedroom apartment for me. My parents' rule was that as long as I was in school and studying or doing an internship, they would support me. I felt a little guilty, since I had an ulterior motive, but I also fully planned to work my butt off at WCP.

Connor Franta and I had become really close at this point and were texting every day. We'd both been dreaming of moving to L.A. for a while, so when I got my internship I asked him if he wanted to come with me, and he said yes! I was psyched to have not just someone to share the journey with but a guaranteed roommate when I got there. My parents had moved to Florida at that point, so Connor flew down to meet me and we packed up the car and started driving. And driving. And driving.

Florida to L.A. is a serious trek, and I don't think there's any way I could have done it on my own. Connor and I took turns driving, got pulled over for speeding, and stayed in the sleaziest motels I've ever seen in my life. We stopped in Texas to pick up Jc, who decided at the last minute that he wanted to come to L.A. too. We somehow found room for all of his stuff along with our own inside my tiny Kia, and made a little cave for him in the middle of all our bags and boxes in the backseat. We got back on the road again and drove until we ran out of gas in the middle of the desert.

I was waiting for the opening credits of a horror movie to start rolling in front of my eyes when I realized I had one bar of cell service on my phone. I was able to call AAA and have someone come rescue us. Crisis (and possible death) averted.

Once we got to L.A., we discovered that the apartment my dad had found was pretty small. Connor and I took the twin beds in the bedroom and Jc claimed the couch in the living room.

We acted like totally dorky tourists for the first few weeks. We hit up every single tourist trap you can think of—the Santa Monica Pier, Huntington Beach, Disneyland, Universal Studios, you name it. If it was pictured on a postcard, we were there.

The reason I had so much time to spare is that my internship only lasted for two weeks.

I dressed up really nice for my first day, thinking that I was heading to an office filled with fancy matching wood and chrome desk sets. Nope, Greg worked out of his house. He wasn't sketchy or anything, but WCP didn't exactly feel like a real company either. It was more like this dude who just sort of picked up freelance gigs whenever he could. He was perfectly nice, though, and we mostly sat around that first day while I showed him my YouTube videos. He said he'd call me the next day and tell me where to go for a shoot that he wanted me to help him with, but I didn't hear from him for six days. I finally got a call and he asked me to come over, but then he just had me sit there on his couch while he fiddled around with camera equipment.

We ended up going off-site on two different days that week, where I was able to help him set up some lighting while he shot an interview for some random online segment. A couple of days later Greg called me to say he was moving his company headquarters and would need to close down for a bit, but he'd call me once he got settled. I never heard from him again.

I was kind of psyched about it. Everything worked out better than I could have hoped; I suddenly had all the free time in the world to work on my videos. I kept my parents updated on the internship—or lack thereof—and prayed that they wouldn't yank me back to the East Coast since I continued to not hear back from Greg. I knew that if I used the free time wisely, I could make enough money to support myself once the internship was technically supposed to be over. And I did!

CHALLENGE

#ASKPERMISSIONFORRICKY

Tell your parents something you've always wanted to do or try but have been too nervous to ask because they might say no. They still might say no, but who knows! Film their reaction or write about it on Twitter.

CHALLENGE

#DRAWMYLIFEFORRICKY

This is a classic for many YouTubers.
Narrate your life story so far using a
dry-erase board for the pictures.

SOCIAL

Oh, Miranda Sings. I love you. I love Colleen Evans, the woman who plays her, even more, though.

I'd been watching Miranda's crazy videos for years, and was borderline obsessed with her. She and Shane Dawson were my everything. Like Shane, Miranda has no boundaries, and I think it was that freedom of creative expression that first drew me to her. Well, that and her penchant for wearing grotesque amounts of red lipstick.

Right around the time I first moved to L.A. with Connor, we got an invite from YouTuber Sawyer Hartman to go to Disneyland for the day with him. We said sure, and that's when he dropped the bomb that Colleen was going to be coming with us. I just about died. DIED.

I had to play it cool. I couldn't come across as just another fan, because I knew in my heart we were destined to become friends, and if I acted like a shrieking geek around her that was never going to happen. I was just going to be one of the gang, no big deal. And somehow secretly get her to know and like me.

When we met up at the front gates and were introduced, I was all, "Oh, hi, nice to meet you. Anyone know the way to Space Mountain?" I pretended she was just any normal person, even though I was doing everything I could not to puke from nerves. That would have been a terrible time for my childhood affliction to flare up again.

But the thing is, she *was* just like any normal person. As we all walked inside the park we began chatting about regular everyday stuff like the weather and traffic. Although, and this is inevitable whenever any two YouTubers get together, the subject of our channels quickly came up. I casually complimented her on hers, trying to keep my voice from cracking with excitement. She, of course, had never heard of mine, but was super interested in talking about it. And I didn't get the feeling that she was just being polite. She seemed genuinely interested in what I was doing and what I had to say.

"We should collab sometime," she said, like it was no big deal.

"Yeah, that would be awesome," I replied, trying not to pee my pants.

The rest of the day flew by. We sat next to each other on all the best rides, like the Haunted Mansion and the Twilight Zone Tower of Terror, and bonded by screaming our heads off. By the time we had to leave I felt like I had made a true friend. But even though we exchanged numbers, a part of me still thought that since she was so cool I'd probably never hear from her again.

Wrong! She reached out almost immediately and invited me over to her house to shoot the videos. When I got there we hung out and gossiped for a little while before getting down to business. It was SO WEIRD to watch Colleen become Miranda! One minute she was the regular, cool girl I'd met at Disneyland, and then before my eyes she transformed into my idol—the narcissistic, clueless yet highly opinionated horrible singer that I loved. The strangest part was seeing her slip in and out of both personalities once she was in Miranda drag.

Hearing her character talk in a normal voice was really bizarre and I couldn't get used to it! It sort of felt like seeing a mall Santa in the parking lot taking a smoke break. The illusion was shattered, but then just as fast she'd slip right back into being Miranda.

The collabs were so fun, but I was definitely nervous at first. I didn't know if I should really amp things up for her to try to make a good impression. Like, do something really crazy. In the end I decided the best road was to just be myself, which ended up being pretty easy—I hardly had to do anything except honestly react to her craziness. She was lightning fast with all her dialogue, which she always ad-libbed on the spot. We'd have to stop the camera a lot because we'd crack up and she would break character. It almost got hard to keep filming because we laughed so much.

For her channel, she taught me how to put on makeup, and of course she did a totally ratchet job. For my channel she gave me a singing tutorial, and I'm sure you can imagine how that went.

I don't even know how many collabs we did after that day. I immediately became part of Miranda's fake boyfriend posse, an honor of the highest degree. We still work together all the time, but even better, I can count Colleen as one of my closest friends. Sometimes she'll invite me and other YouTubers over to her house and we'll spend the whole night playing hide-and-seek in the dark. It's more than sixteen-year-old me ever could have hoped for.

The coolest thing Colleen has taught me is to stay true to myself whenever I'm working with someone on a project. I was still shy around her when I first arrived at her house, and

I could have messed things up big time if I had tried to act like someone I wasn't to try to impress her when we collabed. By acting like myself I got a dear friend *and* a bunch of new viewers, since we combined audiences. Best of both worlds! Ever since that day there have been many times when Colleen and I have hung out and had the best talks. We can literally sit around for hours and the conversation never gets dull. I don't even know if she's aware of this, but she's given me such great advice and encouragement about so many different things when I've needed it. She's a true friend whom I know I can count on, and even more so, just a wonderful, down-to-earth person. Not to mention one of the hardest-working and most creative people I've ever met.

CHALLENGE

#MIRANDAFORRICKY

In honor of the queen herself, take a
selfie in your best Miranda Sings costume.
Make sure to really smear that lipstick!

CHALLENGE

#PIZZAFORRICKY

Buy a premade pizza crust and create the most disgusting pizza you can dream up.

HEALTH

You know what would be so cool? Running a marathon. You know what I have no time to do? Run a marathon.

I knew someone in college who ran one. I watched her train for months for the 26.2-mile big day, and the dedication and focus it took her was insane. People who are new to running are supposed to train for around six months and start out by logging fifteen to twenty miles per week. That's just to *start*. You lose a lot of your social life (and some toenails), plus it's possible to jostle up your insides so much that you might poop your pants halfway through. AND some people's nipples bleed because of shirt chafing. Ouch!

Still, there's something pretty appealing about the satisfaction you must feel after finishing one. Even the word itself—*marathon*—is used as a badge of honor for enduring just about anything.

I've never had one specific goal when it comes to working out except trying to look and feel my best. I think a marathon comes with a lot more complicated feelings. It's all about proving something to yourself, and maybe even your friends and family. There's this idea that if you can complete a marathon, you can handle anything.

Rationally, I know that's not true at all. Anyone can handle anything they want if they try hard enough. Yet the psychological pull is still there. I don't need to climb Mount Everest or swim across the English Channel, I'm happy to leave those crazy missions to the experts. Running a marathon is a doable goal, though, something anyone can accomplish if they try hard enough. I *haven't* tried hard enough, and it nags at me a little. Marathons are often called the hardest physical challenge anyone will ever do, and since, A, I'm all about physical fitness, and B, I'm also all about challenges, a marathon feels like the ultimate goal.

As with any other goal, it takes dedication. Months of it, and that can be a problem. Every single day it's too easy to find a different reason to put it off. There's always an excuse: no time, no energy, you can't miss so-and-so's birthday party, or you need to catch up on *Pretty Little Liars*. I could go on forever. That's the reason that Nike's slogan, "Just do it," is so genius—a lot of the time you have to move beyond motivation and turn training into a reflex.

The thing about a marathon is that it's not about winning, being that first person to break the ribbon at the finish line. Let the people who are trying to beat you at the race have their own kind of fun. It's a whole different experience for them. What I've heard from the less-competitive types like me who've run in one is that marathons are more about building a sense of community. Like, you're all in it together and cheering each other on. Even though I usually like to run alone, that seems pretty cool, since it's happening on such a huge scale. I love the idea of a whole cross section of humanity getting together to achieve this one massive goal as a group. Everyone has their own reasons for wanting to be there, but everyone is united in making it to the end. It's enough to make me tear up.

I don't know what it will finally take for me to get around

to running one. Maybe if there's some sort of solar flare that knocks out the world's electricity and I can't do YouTube anymore I'd find the time. But there I go, making the same excuse everyone has as a reason not to do one—time. I would have to make time, and that's within my control. A big incentive for me is that it would put me in the best shape of my life, and I'd be motivated afterward to maintain that. Or maybe I could get involved with a charity. Raising money for kids with cancer should be motivation enough for anyone.

There's also the matter of bragging rights. If you were one of those kids who were always picked last in gym class, I bet that training and running in a marathon would erase years of dodge ball trauma. If and when I decide to go for it, I think I'd have to start small. Like, maybe a fun run for charity. Then I'd slowly build myself up to where I could handle a half marathon, before tackling the full experience.

CHALLENGE

#RUNFORRICKY

Sign up for a charity run! Don't feel like moving your legs that much? Go hand out water and cheer people on instead!

CHALLENGE

#HUGSFORRICKY

Go up to a stranger and
give him or her a hug.

MUSIC

Back when I was first kicking around the idea of pursuing a music career I decided to test the waters by releasing a cover of "Midnight Memories" by One Direction. Director Andrew Vallentine (you'll hear much more about him later!) helped me film a video for it with Jc and a few other YouTuber friends. I posted it on my channel with a note asking for reactions. The response was phenomenal—there were so many kind comments. Along with some haters, which is to be expected with anything that gets put on the internet, and especially with music, which is a lot more vulnerable than other types of content. I was really happy with the outcome, but had no intention of ever performing the song live. But as it happened, a week after it went up O2L was slated to perform at the O2L tour show with DigiTour in Hawaii, and the producer asked me if I'd perform it on stage. We already had most of our act mapped out. We'd be doing live challenges and Q&As, and Trevor was going to sing, but now suddenly they wanted me to sing, too, and on total impulse I said yes.

At the time I was still deciding what my next step with music should be. Heck, I was still deciding if there should even *be* a next step. Shelby had always told me I had a good voice, and while I know I'm no Ed Sheeran, I have a lot of fun doing it, which is the most important part of any creative journey. Plus

I could already read, write, and understand music thanks to all my years playing the trumpet.

I only had two weeks to get ready to sing live in front of an audience of more than a thousand people. Of course, I promptly lost my voice. Not out of nerves or anything, I legitimately got sick. I tried to conserve my voice as much as possible by not talking and by drinking literally gallons of herbal tea with lemon, like all singers I'd ever seen in movies do.

As the day approached I still wasn't feeling much better, which only added to my nervousness. I knew the rest of the show would be great; the guys and I would be doing things that were within my comfort zone. But as comments kept pouring in on my channel about the 1D cover song, I'd started to get the feeling that maybe I should really try to actively pursue a music career. Suddenly something very real seemed at stake, as opposed to just performing a fun one-off.

Shelby came to Hawaii with me to act as my assistant, so I had a personal cheerleader rooting for me. Of course the O2L guys were all also supportive and psyched for me, but there was something much more special about having a person whom I'd known almost my entire life right there beside me, especially since my voice still wasn't 100 percent back to normal. I was scheduled to perform about twenty minutes into the show, so I had a chance to case the audience and get a feel for the crowd beforehand. I had nothing to worry about there, the energy and love (and SCREAMS) radiating from everyone made me feel like I was in a protective bubble.

I had left the stage for a bit before it was my time to sing because Tyler Oakley was doing a guest appearance Q&A session. As the seconds ticked closer to go-time, Shelby saw the panicked look in my eye and took my hand.

"Hey, relax," she said. "You're about to walk out into a room full of people who already love and support you, and most singers don't get that kind of chance for their big debut. The most important thing right now is for you to have fun with this opportunity that you've been given."

She was right, and I felt a sense of calm settle over me as I walked out on the stage, quickly replaced by a rush of warmth as the crowd cheered. It was hard to make out any individual faces because of all the lights, but that actually made things a little easier. I launched into the song (after letting everyone know I was going to perform it an octave lower than usual because I was still sick) and it was incredible—everyone sang along with me and it felt like we were all in it together. Everyone screamed the chorus and I bounced around the stage, letting all the good vibes wash over me.

If I'm perfectly honest with myself I know that I didn't sound my best, but it was my first time out and taking your first big step is the most important part of any ambitious venture you decide to undertake. You can build on it, and always think to yourself, "Well, at least I was able to do *that* much." After the performance was over the rest of the show seemed to rush by and I was filled with buzzing adrenaline the entire time. Everything around me seemed brighter and funnier, and my entire body felt lighter somehow.

We got to stay in Hawaii for almost a full week after the show, and we celebrated in paradise every day. My favorite experience was snorkeling with my friends on a coral reef off the north shore of Oahu. I was captivated by how beautiful all of the fishes were, and seeing how free they were in such a vast ocean triggered something in me. I felt a deep need to express myself in a way aside from talking and being silly on YouTube. Music is a medium I love and I felt like I could find many different ways to use songs to communicate with the world. And not just by covering other people's lyrics. I began setting plans in motion to record a song of my own, something with a message, something that truly represented me.

CHALLENGE

#SNORKELFORRICKY

I loved being underwater in Hawaii so much that I went so far as to swim with sharks a few years later. (Never again!) If you have an opportunity to, swim with sharks with some professionals! Since that's not a very easily achieved goal, though, try doing it in any body of water. Heck, I'll even settle for a picture of you in a snorkel mask and breathing tube in a kiddie pool. Bonus points if you're holding a tiny plastic shark.

CHALLENGE

#BARKFORRICKY

Pretend that you're a dog or
a cat while out in public.

RANDOM

There used to be a time when brand deals were a dirty little secret of the YouTube business. Maybe *secret* is the wrong word—it's usually pretty obvious when someone is getting paid to hawk a product, but people who did that didn't like to acknowledge what was happening or talk about it at any depth. I think we have all moved beyond that, though. I always make a point of being very transparent when I'm getting paid to promote something. This is how I make a living, and a lot of the money I earn goes directly into funding bigger projects like making an album, music videos, short films, and other creative projects.

On the one hand, I like to keep those two worlds very separate. On the other, I only like to take on a paid project if I can have at least some creative control over it. It's fine if I'm given a few talking points or basic parameters, but I won't do something that's a straight-up advertisement that already has an entire script written for it.

I also have to actually believe in or like a product before I'll do anything with it. A cool pair of sunglasses that I'd wear in a video anyway? Sign me up. Some random ketchup brand? No thanks. I think a lot of people assume that YouTubers say yes to anything that comes their way, but with everyone I know that isn't the case at all. We're actually very selective. I'd say that I probably accept a little less than half of what I get offered.

The first time anyone approached me about promoting a brand was when I moved to L.A. for my internship. I was making a little bit of money from my YouTube channel but not much. Weirdly, the company wanted me to use my Instagram account instead of YouTube. They sent me a cool hoodie for free, and I took a picture of myself wearing it and thanked them in my post. That's it. The reality is I got *paid* to accept a *gift*, as if the gift wasn't enough. It's a weird industry. I genuinely loved the hoodie and it was something I would have worn in a picture naturally anyway, so I felt good about the job.

My first big corporate gig was with Kellogg's. I was kind of intimidated—they're huge! Who doesn't like at least one Kellogg's cereal? What they asked me to do wasn't all that different from the kind of stuff I'd do anyway—yell out a bunch of random things in a crowd, see how many pieces I could toss up into the air and catch in my mouth, and then pick out pieces of different cereals from a bowl with my eyes shut and hands tied behind my back. I hit up a bunch of public places filled with lots of people, like beaches and basketball courts, and screamed that I liked Kellogg's latest chocolate-flavored cereal. It was just a big game.

Deals started rolling in pretty fast after that. I got a gig with Hulu, which was perfect for me because I watch an insane amount of TV and it gave me an excuse to obsessively talk about my favorite shows. Same with Audible. I think it's cool that I can listen to someone read a book while I'm relaxing on a long flight. I love the Harry Potter series and could listen to them over and over a thousand times!

Almost every artist I can think of makes money on the side with advertising deals. Even the ones you would never imagine. Take David Lynch, the awesome weirdo who created *Twin Peaks*. Even after he became famous he directed commercials for Alka-Seltzer and home pregnancy tests on the side! Some famous people do ads to buy, say, a new yacht or a house in the Maldives, but a lot of others, especially musicians and indie filmmakers, use the money to maintain creative control over their work and not have to cave to the demands of a big studio or suck up to a label.

My point is that there's nothing wrong with a little bit of hustling to help you get where you want to go in life. I'm not about to go and get a tattoo of the Golden Palace Casino logo on my forehead like one woman from Salt Lake City did, but I don't see the harm in my giving a paid shout-out every now and then when it helps support my dreams and goals. I don't think anyone should ever be ashamed about how they make money. (Unless it's illegal, obviously.) Our economy is basically a disaster right now, and if there's an opportunity to put food on the table and help me with my videos and music, I'm not going to pass it up.

CHALLENGE

#WORKHARDFORRICKY

Get entrepreneurial and make some extra cash! Host a bake sale, mow a neighbor's lawn, set up a lemonade stand, whatever you want, and show me a picture of you doing your job! It doesn't matter if you only end up making fifty cents, it's the fact that you hustled that counts.

CHAPTER 4

SCARY!!!

CHALLENGE

#PROPOSEFORRICKY

Propose to a stranger—get down
on one knee and offer him or her
a ring from a gumball machine.

FAMILY

'm one of the very few incredibly lucky people out there who have never had a big fight with their family. Seriously, about anything. The worst it ever got was when I'd moan that it was someone else's turn to take out the trash but my mom would make me do it anyway. Boo-hoo, I know.

I am hyperaware that this isn't the case with most kids. I get a lot of comments from my viewers who tell me that they like watching my videos because it helps them escape from their terrible home life. It kills me because I feel like there's nothing I can really do to help them, except keep on making up dance moves that involve shaking my butt and sticking gross things in my mouth to try to make them laugh and forget their problems for a little while.

As supportive of me as my parents have always been, there was one time that I was genuinely scared of their reaction to something: When I decided to tell them that I was dropping out of college and moving to Los Angeles.

No offense to my mom, but I knew that my dad was the one to talk to first. Mom didn't really get YouTube at the time like she does now. She thought it was a fun little hobby I had—not all that different from my filming our family vacations when I was a kid. She definitely supported my making videos, but she didn't see it as anything that might become bigger back then. I knew that if I told her I was discontinuing my higher education to film videos in my bedroom on the other side of the country, she probably would have been on the first flight to L.A. to drag me back home.

My dad, on the other hand, sort of got it. He and I used to always kid about how Mom was never too great with technology. He was much more up to date and in tune with things like the internet and YouTube. He saw the potential in what I was doing, and while I wasn't sure how he'd react when I told him I wanted to make a career out of it, I knew I'd have a better chance of him understanding. But I also knew it could still go either way.

I was supposed to head back home from my internship the first week of August, and while it had always been my secret plan to stay in California, I wanted to really make sure I had enough money flowing in so that I wouldn't be financially dependent on my parents. Otherwise they'd have every right to demand I come back. Luckily, right around mid-July I landed my first few brand deals and sponsorships. I had also started to make just enough from YouTube ad revenue to get by on my own. It was a much-needed boost of confidence that I was making the right decision. Plus, all of the other YouTubers I was meeting were giving me the same advice—that I was at a point with my channel where I had enough subscribers to really have a shot if I decided to commit full-time. It wasn't like I was some starry-eyed kid with nothing in my pockets chasing a dream. None of the YouTubers I knew were irresponsible enough to just tell anyone, "Hey, drop out of your life and move to L.A.!" Their point with me was that I could always decide to go back to school at any point in my life, but I probably wasn't going to have a chance again like the one I currently had, with brand deals starting to roll in and my subscriber base growing steadily on a daily basis. Plus, there were things rolling in that I could only do in L.A., like sketches with Awesomeness TV (that actually aired on their Nickelodeon show!) and a lot of new opportunities with O2L. It would have been really hard to get that sort of momentum again if I went back to school. Plus, having new YouTuber friends whom I admired and looked up to telling me that they believed in me, that I had the potential to become what they were, well, it was downright seductive.

Another issue that was freaking me out about telling my parents was that there was going to be a legitimate problem aside from my disappointment and frustration if my parents said no and tried to force me to come home. O2L had booked a minitour for that October, and if I got stuck in school back in Alabama it would ruin the opportunity for the rest of them.

Connor Franta had recently told his parents that he was staying on the West Coast and they accepted it, which gave me hope. I'd watched all of Joey Graceffa's videos about his decision to drop out of school and move to pursue his dreams. Both of them came through the same experience unscathed and with the full support of their families, and I prayed mine would have the same reaction.

I think it was about three weeks before I was supposed to head home that I decided to finally get it over with and tell Dad my plan. Connor and Jc were both home, so I went out to the backyard and dialed my dad's number. I didn't realize I was holding my breath until he picked up and I suddenly had to talk.

I blurted out my plan to him really fast so I wouldn't

chicken out, and squeezed my eyes shut tight while I waited for him to respond.

"Well, I can't say I didn't see this coming," he said, and I felt my whole body relax.

"Seriously?"

"It's obvious you've been putting a lot of effort into You-Tube," he said. "And I've suspected for a while that this was the direction your life was going in. Your mom and I could both tell how unhappy you were at school last year, and really at the end of the day we just want you to be happy."

I was very relieved, and also filled with gratitude that I had a family who understood me and loved me unconditionally. I told him I didn't expect any handouts, and that I was able to support myself financially. But there was still one last hurdle.

"What about Mom?" I asked.

"Let me talk to her," he said. "I'll help her understand. It's all going to work out, and if for some weird reason it doesn't, you always have a place back here at home."

I felt like crying with joy. I went back inside and threw myself facedown on the couch while Jc and Connor demanded to know how it had gone. After I told them, the three of us went out to dinner to celebrate and toasted to my new life.

CHALLENGE

#CONFESSFORRICKY

Confess something to your parents or
a friend that you've never told them.
Keep it light, though. I don't want anyone
actually getting in trouble! I'm thinking
more like that time you broke a vase when
you were five and blamed it on the dog.

CHALLENGE

#STRANGERSINGFORRICKY

Sing a song to a random stranger.

SOCIAL

ike I said earlier, when I first started watching YouTube, Shane Dawson was everything. (I mean, he still is, but you know what I mean.) He was the undisputed king of YouTube—funny, irreverent, random, sarcastic, but above everything else, TOTALLY relatable. I think all of us early YouTubers aspired to be like him, in that he was so incredibly unique and yet so universal. He said all the self-deprecating things we felt inside but were too afraid to admit.

So when he contacted me out of the blue and asked me to collab with him, I freaked. I'd already been living in Los Angeles for around two months working on my channel, and I knew this was a huge opportunity. But much more important, I was going to meet one of my idols. And HE had asked to meet with ME! I mean, imagine you're a huge Lady Gaga fan and you get an email from her out of the blue asking you to collaborate on a project. My head was basically exploding.

I had actually met him once before at VidCon, but it was part of a huge meet and greet, so I knew he would have no recollection of the moment.

He wanted to film at his house, and I was terrified for days beforehand because I knew his brand of humor. He could be pretty vulgar, and well, not mean, exactly, but pretty blunt. I was scared that he was going to be like that in real life and make fun of me.

He didn't live all that far from our place, so the drive went by really fast. My hands were all sweaty when I rang his doorbell and I half expected him to swing it open and immediately start critiquing my outfit or make fun of my hair.

He didn't, but one of the first things he said to me was, "So what the heck is O2L? Are you guys like the YouTube One Direction? Explain it to me." But he didn't say it in a mean way, he sounded genuinely curious. He'd heard a lot about us but just didn't really understand the concept.

He led me inside as I explained what we were about. I tried not to be obvious as I scoped out his place—everything was very clean and modern. I also had to keep myself from acting like a total fanboy. I couldn't believe I was actually talking to Shane in person, in his own private territory.

We sat down on the couch and ended up chatting for over an hour before we even started filming. It was definitely scary at first, but pretty soon I relaxed into it and before long we were talking like we were old friends, laughing at all the same stuff and bonding over how weird it could be sometimes to be a YouTuber.

He had tweeted to his fans that I was coming over to collab and asked them for suggestions about what we should do. A lot of them knew who I was and knew I was a pretty innocent and clean guy. So of course he chose "sexual Mad Libs." All the stories were themed around sleepovers. It was definitely a departure for me, but also sort of freeing. Since it wasn't going to be on my channel, I felt like I could be a little more risqué than I usually am. My adjectives and nouns were nowhere near as gross as Shane's, but I definitely branched out and tried to keep up without being too offensive. (I'm not going to repeat any of it here, but you can easily go watch the video if you're curious.)

Since that collab ended up being so raunchy I dialed everything down several notches for the collab that would appear on my channel. I chose to do the Jenga Challenge, a game invented by Joey Graceffa where a bunch of the Jenga pieces have different condiments and liquids written on them, stuff like horseradish, mustard, and baby food. You have to eat a spoonful of whatever you pull, and whoever knocks the tower down has to combine ALL the ingredients listed on the blocks into a blender and drink it. I was doing pretty well (and keeping things G-rated despite Shane's best efforts to make everything sound sexual), but unfortunately I got a little too excited and hit the table. The entire tower tumbled down, and here's the final recipe I had to drink:

clam juice
beef baby smoothie
tartar sauce
mustard
horseradish
powdered lemonade
mayonnaise
hot sauce
chocolate syrup
FREAKIN' SARDINES WITH THE HEADS STILL ATTACHED

We blended it all and topped the nastiness with whipped cream. Guys, I tried to drink the whole thing. I really did. I wanted to impress you and Shane with my bravado, but I spat out the first mouthful almost immediately. I sucked up all my courage, held my breath, and took an actual gulp, and that's as far as I got. It tasted like toxic waste mixed with diarrhea and rotting fish, and while I love my viewers, I have my limits. Remember, I used to have a vomiting problem.

By the time we cleaned up and I left Shane's house I knew I'd made a new friend for life. We started texting a lot, and as my channel grew I constantly asked him for career advice and he always gave wise answers. I still consider him someone I can turn to whenever I have questions or need someone to talk to if I'm feeling upset. The whole experience was just like meeting Colleen for the first time—I was terrified to meet my idol, but not scared enough to feel like I had to change who I am.

I wish I'd had that same self-confidence back when I was in high school. There were plenty of people whom I thought were really cool and I would have loved to be friends with, but I never had the guts to talk to them. I know this scenario with Shane is a little different because he is the one who actually invited me over, but I think no matter what, if you have people up on a pedestal, chances are they won't be as hard to reach as you think. Whenever I talk to someone about meeting Shane for the first time I tell that person how pleasantly surprised I was at how nice and down to earth he is. Not that I expected him to be a bad person or anything, it's just that he's honestly one of the nicest people I've met from YouTube. Even though we've gotten to be close friends, I still really look up to him as both a person and a content creator. He's one of the coolest guys I've had the pleasure of getting to know. Hi, Shane! If you're reading this, I hope it isn't too awkward. But hey, read this in one of those videos you do where you make fun of You-Tuber books! I'd be honored.

CHALLENGE

#NASTYSMOOTHIEFORRICKY

That's right—re-create this exact same drink and take at least one real sip. No cheating, I want to see you blend it!

CHALLENGE

#HOTSAUCEFORRICKY

Gather up as many different kinds of
hot sauces as you can and try them all.
(Here's a tip for after—milk works better
than water for getting rid of the burn!)

HEALTH

For professional athletes, there's nothing more terrifying than a career-destroying injury. For fifteen-year-old Ricky Dillon, there was nothing more terrifying than a bunch of seniors thinking I couldn't deadlift as much weight as they could.

See where I'm going with this?

After I'd finally made the varsity tennis team my sophomore year of high school, we had about a month to prep before the season started, and a lot of that time was meant for weight training to help build up our arms. I remember walking into the gym after school and seeing a bunch of buff senior dudes grunting and picking up two-hundred-pound weights as if they were feather pillows.

Since I'd had such a hard time making the team, I felt like I needed to prove myself to these guys. Never mind that no one had ever taught me how to lift correctly, or even told me that you were supposed to have a spotter. I just wanted to show these total strangers that I was worthy of playing tennis alongside them. If that meant defying gravity by picking up a hunk of lead that really didn't want to move from where it was already resting comfortably, then I was going to go for it.

I don't remember how much weight I tried to lift. All I can recall is standing over the barbell, sneaking a glance in the mirror to make sure people were watching, and then bending over.

Next came the searing pain in my back as a hunk of muscle tore away from my spine.

I went straight to the school's trainer and told him what had happened. By then the pain was already fading, but it was replaced by the horrifying sensation of strained muscle rubbing up against bone with every step I took. Every tiny movement reminded me that something INSIDE MY BODY had come loose.

I was fully healed a month later when tennis season started, but only barely in time. I had to do a full month of physical therapy, including gentle workouts on this weird machine that made my arms spin around like legs do on a stationary bike. I also had to constantly swap out cold compresses throughout the day. It was so embarrassing. I couldn't decide whether I felt more like an old man with my bad back, or like a child because of my dumb thought that I could do anything the big kids did.

I'm very, very careful now in the gym. Almost to the point of paranoia, but the good kind that means you're watching out for yourself. As soon as I was able to pick things up again after the accident, I made sure to learn the proper form and technique for every kind of lifting out there. And now I never, ever do any sort of really heavy lifting at the gym without a spotter by my side.

I almost threw away all my years of hard work and practice to get onto the tennis team because I was scared about making an impression on some total strangers. It's horrifying for me to think about now, but I also still understand why that self-consciousness exists in teenagers and adults alike. I used to have tons of gym anxiety. Gyms can be scary, intimidating places, which sucks because the whole reason they exist is so you can feel good about yourself. Whether you're dealing with machine hogs or scarily beautiful people who look like their bodies are sculpted out of marble, you have to remember that they do not matter. When you are at a gym, *you* are the only one who matters. You're taking positive steps so you can live a longer and fuller life. You have to find a way to not see the people that make you uncomfortable. Don't be jealous of the person with abs you could break a nail on. Ask the person how he got them! In my experience people who aren't wearing headphones at the gym are usually more than happy to talk or answer any fitness questions you have. You might even make a new friend. But leave them alone if they have their headphones on; that's usually a good sign that they don't want to be bothered.

CHALLENGE

#SPOTFORRICKY

Go to a gym (or *the* gym, if you're in school) with a friend and take turns spotting each other while lifting weights. If you've never

done this before, make sure to
ask a staff member or your gym
teacher to teach you the proper
techniques first, and go light!

#AUTOGRAPHFORRICKY

Go up to a stranger and freak out,
pretending the person is a celebrity.
Ask for a selfie and get his or her
autograph. Extra love if you get a friend
to film it, and even more love if the
person actually *looks* like a celebrity.

SELF-EMPOWERMENT

After my dad gave me the go-ahead to remain in L.A., I knew the next step was finding a real home. Sharing a room in Westwood with Connor was fun but the setup was basically a dorm. Plus at that point both Kian and Jc had moved into the living room. Four boys, less than five hundred square feet, and one bathroom doesn't stay fun for very long.

My lease on the place was up at the end of July, since that's when my dad originally thought I'd be returning to Alabama, so we had to move fast since I'd waited so long to get permission to stay. The only place we could find on such short notice that had room enough for all of four of us was all the way out in Encino, almost a full hour away from all the best parts of L.A.

This was right when the O2L channel started really blowing up, and the place quickly became known as the O2L house. Trevor and Sam didn't officially live there, but they were over all the time. That house was the background for many of our videos, had its own Twitter account, and Jc posted a sixty-second tour that racked up over a million views.

Connor and I both really liked our alone time after a long day, while Jc and Kian were super social. Jc loved to have people over and throw parties, and they were both also really, really into playing pranks. And not just for videos to post. One day I woke up to find that they'd tied my bedroom's outside doorknob to another one in the hallway, so I was locked in my room. It was funny at first, then annoying, then *really* annoying when I realized I was going to be late for an important meeting.

The entire year is sort of a blur in my memory because everything was happening so fast in terms of our career. Thank God most of it is on YouTube so it's chronicled. When our lease was up we knew that we wanted to live closer to L.A., and that's when Connor decided to move out and get his own place. It wasn't anything dramatic—he was like me and just preferred a quieter environment. He was ready to step out on his own, but I wasn't quite there yet. I needed a little more time to adjust to my new life, and I liked having the support of roommates. Jc and Kian made me feel safe (even with the pranks).

Our next place was weird. The house itself was cool—it was located in the Hollywood Hills, had an awesome pool and hot tub, and even a secret little room hidden behind a huge mirror near the kitchen. There were only two problems with it. The first was that my bedroom was located right off the front door, so I'd hear everything and not be able to sleep any time Jc and Kian had friends over. The other problem was our landlord. He was nuts. He'd show up at random times and yell at us about nothing. There was also a huge freak-out when the guys dared me to jump off the roof and into the pool. Apparently the neighbors filmed it and called the landlord and he bugged out, saying that it was against the law (it isn't) and that I was trying to hide it from him (I wasn't; it was already posted online).

I'd been living in L.A. for close to two years at that point, and I finally felt brave enough to branch out on my own. I could be just as social as Jc and Kian, but I'm the kind of person who very much needs an equal amount of quiet time. Living in a house with other guys made it hard sometimes. I love them all to death, but sometimes I just need to be completely alone after a long day. It helps me stay productive and sane.

That being said, I don't know whether I would have lasted had I moved to L.A. by myself. It was so good to have roommates to help me adjust and grow comfortable in a new city, especially ones as amazing as Jc, Kian, and Connor. They gave me the confidence to grow and finally head out solo.

I knew I wanted to live in a loft, and it didn't take me long to find the perfect one in Venice, near the ocean but not too far away from the city. It was the perfect escape, a nest I could come home to after a long day of shooting collabs, recording music, or having important meetings and just chill out on the couch. I could watch all the TV in the world I wanted without worrying that a party was about to roll through the door at any moment. And no one tried to lock me in my bedroom anymore.

The rest of the boys ended up moving out of the other house, too, right around the same time I did. Not because they wanted alone time, but because apparently some big scary dudes in suits showed up at the front door asking them where the landlord was. They told them they had no idea, and that's when the men started telling them about all the money the landlord owed them and that they'd better tell him he was in big trouble. It felt way too Mafia, and they cleared out fast.

Someone by your side when creepy guys show up at the front door is just one of the million reasons why having roommates is awesome. Throwing dinner parties and having someone to talk to in the middle of the night when you can't sleep, not to mention sharing bills, make that first step into adulthood that much easier. Living with other people can lead to some of the best friendships you'll ever have. I was so lucky to have such a strong support system while I built my career. I don't regret one second of living with them. It created some of the best memories I think I'll ever have in my life. Best of all, I can now fully appreciate the pleasure of coming home to a blissfully silent place, knowing I can walk around naked and no one will care.

CHALLENGE

#KNJPRANKFORRICKY

Climb up onto your roof and jump into the pool. **KIDDING!** Do not do that. I repeat, do not do that. Instead, pull the same prank that Kian and Jc played on me by tying someone's door shut from the outside. Just be sure to let him or her out pretty quick. Trust me, it sucks if you don't.

CHALLENGE

#BUNDLEUPFORRICKY

**Put on as many layers of clothing
as you can and post a selfie.**

MUSIC

About a month after I debuted "Midnight Memories," I followed it up with a cover of "Don't Say Goodnight" by Hot Chelle Rae, and the response was just as great. When I was a kid, one of my biggest dreams was to be a singer, but I'd kept it a secret. It was just something I'd never thought possible until YouTube came into my life. And while I'd already succeeded at vlogging beyond any of my wildest hopes, I knew I'd probably need a little professional help to make becoming a professional singer a reality.

I'd known Charlie Puth socially from the YouTube circuit for a long time, and we'd been friends for a while, long before I even moved to L.A. He's such a pro and I knew from the start that he was destined for huge things. (I was right—that song he did with Wiz Khalifa for the *Furious 7* soundtrack now has over one BILLION views on YouTube!) He was already working with O2L on a song, and when I casually asked him if he'd be willing to collaborate on a song with me he said yes! The idea of writing an original song was terrifying but I knew I was in great hands. Charlie is a natural genius with music, not to mention patient and kind.

Since I didn't really know anything about the music industry at the time, I didn't know what to expect. I had no idea whether he'd be able to understand the idea that I could see so clearly in my head, but didn't have the know-how to get out. I had nothing to worry about, though—he made the whole process feel natural and seamless. We hung out for a whole day in my bedroom at the Encino house, talking and playing around on my computer with GarageBand. I wanted the song to be really pop-y and fun, something you could just put on and jam to, and I also knew exactly what I wanted it to be about—the fact that you can have fun without drinking or doing drugs. It's okay to be "Ordinary" and not always feel like you have to be crazy and follow the crowd. Being your own ordinary self is even cooler! The song was pretty much a direct response to my monklike ways in high school and college, but also something I totally still believe. You can be normal and sober and still have a blast. It's weird how so many songs are about the exact opposite—people getting hammered and name-checking liquor and champagne brands. Not that I've got anything against those kinds of songs, it's just that I'd never heard something that was fun and had the opposite message.

Charlie came up with an amazing melody and words for the chorus, and I wrote a lot of the lyrics in the verses with Charlie's help. In case anyone's wondering, the Kia Soul reference was NOT product placement. I genuinely love my old car! They *should* have paid me for that shout-out. J/K! But not really. Hey, Kia, you're welcome for all that free promotion!

We recorded the next day, and suddenly I had a song of my very own! Looking back after making so much music since, the entire process was lightning fast. It's crazy how quickly we made the song—then again, Charlie is a musical genius.

What I needed next was a video, and I really loved all the

ones that Joey Graceffa had been putting out. The production values were always out-of-this-world good, and he introduced me to his director, that guy Andrew Vallentine whom I mentioned earlier, the one who helped me with "Midnight Memories." We met up and I told him I wanted my video to be as light and fun as the song. He came up with the general concept on the spot. We rented this adorable barn with a movie-ready field made for frolicking in, and I recruited a bunch of friends like Kian, Jc, and jennxpenn to dance around and act silly with.

From start to the finished release, the whole thing took us less than two weeks. That time frame ended up setting a bad example for me, and unrealistic expectations for future music projects. I thought all songs and videos would come together just as fast and easily, but I'd soon learn that was hardly the case. I got lucky, big time.

After I posted the video the response from viewers was very supportive and loving, but my favorite memory of the whole experience is that day I had dancing around with my friends in the sun in the middle of a meadow. I think you can see it on our faces, too; nothing about filming it ever felt forced. It was like the song had actually come to life around me! I'm so happy that it's preserved on film forever. I had no idea at the time that it was only the first step of a massive journey that I'm still on.

The idea of seriously pursuing a music career was scary, but I listened to my fear and tried to examine what it was really about. Genetically, I think we experience fear as a survival mechanism, a big red flag that something dangerous is happening. But since we're not being chased by woolly mammoths anymore, I think fear has evolved into many different things. Conquering a fear when it comes to reaching out for what you want out of life equals emotional growth, which is just as important to survival as not getting eaten.

CHALLENGE

#ORDINARYFORRICKY

Make a music video to "Ordinary."
No rules here—you can lip-sync
it or sing it yourself, just show
me your vision for the song.

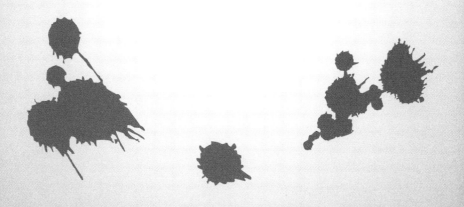

CHALLENGE

#STRANGERDANCEFORRICKY

Convince a stranger to

slow-dance with you.

RANDOM

Now let's take fear to a very literal place—scary movies! It's weird that my first serious leap into acting was for my first original short film, *The Storybook Killer*, because I'm actually terrified of certain types of horror flicks.

For years I'd wanted to shoot a big Halloween video for my channel, but I'd always remember that plan about three days before October 31, so I'd never have time. This past year I remembered a little bit earlier, but only by, like, two weeks. I met up with Andrew Vallentine and we volleyed some ideas around and decided we should make an actual movie instead of just some sort of themed-prank video.

We got my friend Whitney Milam to write the script for us, and I knew I wanted to cast YouTubers, so I brought on Meg DeAngelis and Josh Leyva, but I also wanted seasoned actors in it to give it a little more cred, and we landed Ashley Argota, who has been all over Nickelodeon, the Disney Channel, and more recently a show I personally adore called *The Fosters*. We also got Cody Saintgnue, who's best known for his recent role in another show I love, *Teen Wolf*.

The story centers on two brothers, one of whom disappears at a creepy theme park based on fairy tales like Sleeping Beauty and Snow White. On the tenth anniversary of the brother's disappearance, a mysterious note shows up that leads the surviving brother and his friends to the park, where they get slaughtered one by one.

I can deal with serial killer movies. In fact, the *Halloween* series is one of my favorite franchises ever. Even the lamer sequels like the one where a reality TV company run by Busta Rhymes and Tyra Banks locks a bunch of kids up in Michael Myers's house totally does it for me. My thinking is that if you're dealing with a crazy killer on the loose, you can make decisions based on real life to get out of the situation.

But if you've got a demon or a ghost on your hands, forget it. Movies like *The Exorcist*, *The Ring*, *Evil Dead*, and *Paranormal Activity* are on my permanent banned list. There's just something deeply unsettling and unnerving to me about creatures that are otherworldly.

Look, I know we're just talking about movies here, but they seriously scare me! The few times I've managed to sit through an entire ghost movie, I wasn't able to sleep for days. Give me Jason Voorhees any day and I know I'd stand a chance as long as there was a machete nearby. The one exception to my rule about paranormal subjects is the show *Supernatural*. If there's comedy involved, it helps take away the creepiness of demon possession.

Anyway, back to *The Storybook Killer*. Luckily Whitney's script didn't call for any ghost stuff. We filmed it at an actual theme park called Enchanted Forest in Oregon, a cool little tourist trap filled with plaster castles and doorways that look like you're walking into a witch's mouth. It's a pretty eerie place, and felt even more so because it was closed for the winter at the time—perfect for our plot about the place being abandoned.

Getting to see everything that goes on behind the scenes of a horror movie makes it seem anything but scary, though. Watching the makeup and special effects people work their magic took away any element of fear. There are some majorly gory things that happen, but we were all laughing and joking as our brilliant makeup artist Monique Paredes applied tons of fake blood. Seeing how it was done took away any power the moment might have had over me if I were simply a viewer. It's a good thing to remember if you're watching a horror movie and get scared. If you see any blood, just remember that there's probably a production assistant desperate for a lunch break holding a bucket of the sticky red dye just offscreen, ready to apply more gore if needed.

I came away from the whole experience with a couple of thoughts. One: I want to act in more films! Man, it was fun! But more important, there are a lot more things in this world to be scared of than a fictional movie. Acne and red carpet wardrobe malfunctions—these are worthy of my fear. A computer-generated poltergeist is not.

CHALLENGE

#SCREAMFORRICKY

**Let's hear your best
horror movie scream!**

CHAPTER 5

FUN

CHALLENGE

#WRONGSHOESFORRICKY

Wear a different shoe on each foot and
tally up how many people actually point
it out to you during an entire day.

MUSIC

kept on working with Andrew Vallentine on almost all of the music videos I put out. The most involved one we did for the songs on the EP I put out after recording "Ordinary" was for "Stars." I wanted to film it at some sort of barren, alien landscape, and after he did some research he came up with the idea of shooting in Iceland! He showed me photos of all these eerie black beaches, which were perfect. Normally our crew on a video could run as high as sixty people, but since Iceland was so far away (er, expensive), there were only five of us on location. Normally I'll spare no cost when it comes to music videos. I'll take on extra brand deals so I make sure that the final picture matches my initial inspiration. But we're talking about Iceland . . . there was no way I could hustle up enough extra cash to get a giant team there.

It worked out better that way. Having fewer people around gave me a much better feel for the sense of isolation there, and I think it shows. With such a small team, we were able to travel all over instead of being confined to one place.

Andrew had flown there a week early to scout locations, and when the rest of us arrived we hopped in a rental car and drove along the southern coast to all the different spots he'd found, and we stayed in a different motel each night.

Everywhere we went, locals told us that we should have come to visit in the summer, that it was much more beautiful then. I felt their point—it was freezing! We filmed at a hot spring that was anything but and was surrounded by snow. When we shot a scene at a waterfall, the splashback felt like a million tiny needles on my skin. The coldest moment of my life was having to strip out of my costume behind a wall to change back into normal clothes. I swear I had hypothermia! Sometimes there were fifty-mile-an-hour winds that you could literally lean into and they would keep you standing. But it was all so worth it—I'll do anything and go anywhere for the perfect shot, and I don't think we could have gotten the same sort of incredible landscape scenes if it had been nice out. All of the spooky weather enhanced the exact atmosphere we were going for. (Still, I'd love to go back sometime and experience those hot springs the way they're meant to be!)

At the time it was the biggest project I'd ever taken on, and it's definitely one of the best trips I've ever been on.

When it came time to shoot the video for my next song, I wanted something completely different, and as usual Andrew was down.

I really love videos that are filmed in one long, continuous shot, like "Start All Over" by Miley Cyrus and "Hideaway" by Kiesza, and I wanted to try something like that for "BEAT," the first single I released after putting out my EP, *RPD*. The song is inspired by my time in marching band, so it made sense to me to have the movements keep on going and going, just like we used to have to do at games. Instead of a football field, the vision I had was people dancing with me in a dark alleyway in a mysterious city at night. The only problem: I wasn't that great a dancer. So we hired a choreographer named Mike Munich who has worked with Lady Gaga, and he was brilliant. He created a bunch of moves that I could learn easily and look good doing. We practiced together for a week before the actual shoot, which took place on a Disney back lot where things like *Pirates of the Caribbean* and episodes of *Grey's Anatomy* had been shot.

We booked an all-night shoot, from 6:00 p.m. to 6:00 a.m., and filming it was more like being in a play than being in a video, since we kept going in a single shot for so long. In truth it's three continuous shots edited together to look like one. Our choreographer hired all of these incredible backup dancers—one of them had been in three Beyoncé videos *and* toured with her! These people were professionals, and I most definitely was not. I was completely nervous and freaked out. I thought they'd be like, *Who is this kid?* They couldn't have been nicer or more supportive, though, and we'd laugh and joke around between takes, even when the sun started to rise and we were all exhausted.

I'm really happy with how it came out. I keep pushing myself harder and harder when it comes to making videos, but it never feels like work. At the time I'm writing this I just finished shooting with Trevor Moran for the song I did with him, "Steal the Show," from my album *Gold*. My plan is to make a video for every single song on there (and spread them out over time, of course). Since I rented a freaking rain machine for the video with Trevor, I'm starting to feel like I need to either keep out-doing myself (shoot something at the bottom of the ocean!) or take it down a few notches (Ricky Unplugged?). Whatever I decide, I promise to make it fun for you.

CHALLENGE

#CHOREOFORRICKY

Create your own choreographed
dance routine to "**BEAT.**" It doesn't
have to be to the entire song. I
just want to see you move!

CHALLENGE

#BENICEFORRICKY

**Make someone's day and give a
stranger a genuine compliment.**

HEALTH

I hope I haven't been sounding too preachy every time I write about fitness. I don't mean to, it's just that staying in shape changed my attitude and the way I feel about myself so much that I want everyone in the world to get the same kind of benefits out of it that I do. The last thing I want, though, is to come across as some sort of barking gym teacher when all you really want to be doing is binge-watching *Scream Queens* for the fourth time.

But. BUT! You can do both!

What I'm about to suggest here is hardly revolutionary, I don't even think they make treadmills without TVs on them anymore. If you don't want to leave the house, then don't! As much time as I spend running and working out at the gym, I think I get some of my most important and consistent work done in the privacy of my own home zoning out to the soothing sounds of the Kardashian/Jenner sisters.

Sit-ups. Push-ups. Crunches. Squats. Leg lifts. Planking. Lunges. Calf lifts. Floor humps.

Okay, I made that last one up, but these are all really easy exercises to do while hanging out alone in your living room. They don't require any equipment, they're free, and they're relatively hard to screw up. If it's tough for you to complete a push-up, turn on Fox News and scream your way through a couple.

Still too much exertion for you? Pick up one of those little hand squeezy thingies. (Googling those words will get you to what I'm talking about—apparently the technical term is "handgrips.") Invest in an inflatable yoga ball and watch TV upside down while stretching your back, or sit on it and bounce gently up and down to strengthen your core. Heck, buy a Hula Hoop and shimmy your hips while watching *Ellen*! It's low-impact cardio that helps slim your waistline. Just watch out for vases on nearby end tables.

The average American watches at least five hours of TV a day, and if Netflix keeps churning out more original programming, that number is only going to go up. Even if you stayed active for just one of those five hours you'd be ahead of the game.

Think about how much exercise you used to get as a little kid just playing on the playground, and you had no idea that what you were doing was good for you.

As an adult, you have to learn how to enjoy exercise in that same way in order for it to ever become a part of your day-to-day life. If you truly hate exercising, then the trick is finding the fun in it. And if that is totally impossible for you, then you need to create some sort of reward system. Are you a huge music freak and have to hear everything that Spotify releases on Fridays? Don't let yourself unless you've got a barbell in your hand (just make sure that you've threaded your headphone wires under your shirt). Or maybe you're one of the .99 percent of the population that hasn't read the *Hunger Games* trilogy and you just got an audio download of the third book. Don't press play until you've sat down on a rowing machine.

Here's another tactic. You know that friend you love but you never see anymore because you're both too busy? Create a buddy system and make a weekly date to go for a run. It can be your special time to reconnect *and* tighten your butts! Connor and I love to do this sometimes when we hang out.

The friend doesn't *have* to be someone you don't see often. Working out with any friend increases the odds that you'll continue. You can push each other to do better, and each promise to always force the other out of the house when one isn't feeling it. Not to mention it's literally social time so it just becomes fun naturally.

If you know that you aren't into a specific kind of exercise, like tennis, and you have friends who are super into tennis and are always trying to get you to play with them, don't do it. If you don't enjoy something, you're not going to continue it. Spend the time that your friends are off doing their thing to find some kind of physical activity that YOU love. That being said, it is important to try new things, so if a pal invites you to try out a sport that you've never played before, at least give it a shot! Even if you end up not liking it, you still got in a good workout and hung out with friends.

One cool thing to keep in mind is that exercise can be almost anything you want it to be. Frisbee is exercise! Long walks on the beach are exercise! Playing tag is exercise! Walking a dog is exercise! Hopping up and down in your bedroom for five minutes is exercise! Best of all, dancing is exercise. Hit up a club or a school dance, and if you don't live near a place to go dancing, get Dance Dance Revolution and invite a bunch of friends over to do that on a Friday night. If you don't have any friends or a video-game system, take a cue from Robyn and keep on dancing on your own. That's what I love to do—blast music alone in my room and dance while I clean it. I don't think my room would ever get clean if I couldn't dance while doing it.

If you've got a boyfriend or a girlfriend then you're in luck, because working out with a significant other (as long as you're past the whole I'm-too-scared-to-let-him-or-her-see-me-sweat phase) can be a great bonding process. It gets your hearts racing, you have alone time together, and you're motivating each other to look and feel better.

If you're still not buying any of this, look at the data. I mean, I don't have it here, but look it up online. There are a million different studies that prove how much exercise can help improve your overall mood. Our bodies are made to move around and grow muscle, not sit around and collect weight. It's like a crime against nature to not take advantage of these crazy bags of flesh that we live in. I know there's only so much convincing I can do, and by no means am I trying to force any of this on you. I'm simply hoping to inspire, because fitness is such a positive part of my life and I love seeing it change other people's lives, too. In the end you are the only one who can convince yourself to work out. But I swear to you on everything I hold dear—if you can learn to make it fun, working out regularly will be one of the best things you can do for yourself.

CHALLENGE

#TVWORKOUTFORRICKY

Make up a new, creative way to work out while watching TV. It can be absolutely anything, as long as some part of your body is moving. The weirder the moves, the better.

CHALLENGE

#BLINDFOLDMAKEUPFORRICKY

Do the blindfold makeup challenge
(blindfold yourself and a friend
and trust each other to do your
faces up) and post the results.
Extra love if you go out in public.

FAMILY

know I've mentioned my friend Shelby a lot, and I think she deserves her own little section for being my sister from another mister.

Anyway, she's family, no question. I talk with her every single day, and we've known each other since kindergarten, when I tried to fix her broken marriage with my friend Thomas. They were hitched in that way kids pretend to be, but she'd broken up with him on Valentine's Day because he drew her a card with a picture of a fish on it. It was a classic communication breakdown situation: Shelby hated fish, but had never mentioned that fact to Thomas, who only knew how to draw one thing well, which happened to be fish. So much *drama* with young love!

Thomas came to me incredibly upset over what had happened and begged me to talk to her for him. So I did, but I wasn't able to do much good. The damage had been done, but at least it put Shelby on my radar.

Even though she lived only a few streets over, and we even had lockers next to each other in sixth grade, we didn't become close until middle school, when we were both in band. She was first-chair flute, and we both attended a summer band camp program at the local college. When her mom dropped her off on the first day, she yelled out to me from the car that I needed to look out for Shelby, so I did!

We started doing everything together. Well, as much as two people who don't party can do in Alabama, which it turns out isn't much. We were both obsessed with *American Idol* and would watch it live and vote. Any time a franchise movie like *Harry Potter* or *Twilight* premiered we'd be waiting in line at the first midnight screening, and would sometimes go to the twenty-four-hour gym at 3:00 a.m. so we could work out and have the place to ourselves and be as loud as we wanted.

We also spent a lot of time just driving around and talking. One day we decided to take a road trip to the ocean, and right before we left she won a little stuffed monkey from a vending machine and hung it from her rearview mirror. She called it her Lucky Monkey. It was anything but. She got pulled over for speeding, and we got hopelessly lost, so she ended up throwing the animal out the window after yelling at it for being an Unlucky Monkey.

Band trips were much more fun, since we didn't have to worry about driving. The school would charter a bus for away games and we always made sure to sit next to each other and play Mario Kart on our Nintendo DSes. Some football games ended up being super far away, so we had some trips that were fifteen-hour bus rides. I remember the first one vividly. We were freshmen and sat together and bonded even more than ever before. We really do have band to thank for getting us so close.

Since we didn't march in the same section, we'd always scramble to find each other whenever we had a break. It was always a struggle, since all two hundred band members looked EXACTLY the same in our uniforms, especially when we had to warm up in a dark parking lot near the field.

Shelby and I even dated on and off. It was never anything serious, we'd just sort of slip into being a couple, and just as quickly go right back to normal. It wasn't weird to either of us because we were already so tight. I think we both just realized that we make for perfect friends instead of a couple. But who knows, we could end up getting married someday!

When I was recording my album it was her idea to sing together on "Got Your Back." We'd spent countless hours singing together in the car when we were younger so I thought I really knew her voice, but I was surprised at how great it was when she focused. When she sang in the car it was a bit more reserved, but she fully opened up in the studio and did a fantastic job, especially considering it was her first time doing any sort of singing on a professional level. It's one of my favorite songs on *Gold*!

She's finishing up college at UAB in Alabama now and plans on moving to L.A. as soon as she graduates. Her plan is to become a manager or publicist or something similar in the social media world. I've definitely got her back on that.

CHALLENGE

#BFFFORRICKY

Post a picture of your best friend—
doesn't matter if it's someone you've
known since kindergarten, your mom,
your pet fish, or your laptop.

CHALLENGE

#THANKFULLISTFORRICKY

Make a list of all of the things
you're thankful for in life and put it
in a place where it's easy to look at
whenever you're feeling down.

SELF-EMPOWERMENT

I can count the number of girlfriends I've had on just over one hand, and all except one were during high school. There was always this sort of unspoken pressure to date at mine. It was the social norm, so if you weren't dating anyone, you looked and felt kind of out of place. Therefore, I sort of went along with whatever came my way. I don't want to say I didn't have a good time with any of them, or that the relationships were fake, but they definitely weren't something I would have necessarily sought out. More thoughts on that later.

My first girlfriend was named Lucy, and we got together when I was in ninth grade. She was on one of the off-campus tennis teams with me, and had a great energy. We had crushes on each other but I doubt I would have acted on it if her friends hadn't seriously pressured me into asking her out. It felt forced at first, but we ended up being together for eight months. The problem was that her schedule was really busy, so we only ever saw each other at school and during practice. We hung out with big groups of people but never had any alone time. We finally called it off when it was clear it was going nowhere, but we stayed friends.

Girlfriend number two was my first kiss! She's also now married to Mason. I first met Chelsea one night when I went out bowling with Mason my sophomore year. One of his friends had invited her, and we instantly connected and talked nonstop the whole night. It was the start of spring break and I was heading off to my family's lake house for the week the next day, but we exchanged numbers and continued to text and talk the whole time I was gone. I couldn't believe how much we had in common. She was on the tennis team and played really well, but for some reason we'd just never talked. She also loved singing, and way before I ever made my own YouTube channel I helped her set one up for herself so she could record covers of songs and upload them. I was kind of like her unofficial manager/videographer.

There was a trail that led up into the woods behind her house, and that's where I had my first kiss. It should have been perfect—warm weather, a bright moon shining down, a soft wind that rustled the leaves—it was a textbook first-kiss scenario.

Instead of appreciating all that, I got kind of weirded out. I felt like things were moving too fast, like she was suddenly already planning our whole future. We still gave the relationship another good four months before eventually breaking up because she thought things were moving too slow. In hindsight, dating in general has just always freaked me out for some reason, so I couldn't keep up with the normal dating pace that she naturally wanted to go at. It wasn't an awkward breakup; we stayed friends, and a month later both she and Mason needed a date for homecoming, so I set them up. The rest is history.

Junior year brought Juliana into my life, and I honestly don't remember why she didn't work out. It was good at first but for one reason or another we just broke up. From the start, though, it had never been too serious, so it was no big deal.

I'd known Mallory for years, but we didn't get together until my senior year. I was interested in becoming a drum major (the person who conducts the marching band) and she had been one so she started coaching me. One thing led to another and then we were dating, but she'd had a serious boyfriend before me whom she still had feelings for, and they eventually got back together.

All through high school Shelby and I had been doing our friends/sometimes more thing on and off, but by the time we graduated we were definitely in the permanent friend zone. But, like, in the good kind of friend zone.

My final girlfriend lasted two weeks my freshman year of college. We both played trumpet in band so we were together all the time and it seemed like the right thing to do. It wasn't. I guess we just kind of jumped the gun with dating. It was too sudden, and then we realized, *Wait, this feels weird*. As with all my other exes, we stayed friends. (Good thing, since we had to sit next to each other every day.) I feel really lucky that I've managed to stay friendly with all of my ex-girlfriends. I've never had any bad feelings about our breakups.

I know what you're probably thinking. *Ricky, are you sure you aren't gay?* It wouldn't be the first time I've heard it, but it's usually used as an insult, which is pathetic since there's nothing wrong with being gay so it doesn't even work as a slur.

It's actually insane just how dramatic and overly discussed the topic of my sexuality gets in the comments section of my YouTube videos, in my Instagram feed, and on Twitter. The fact of the matter is, it's not even a big deal to me. I hardly ever even think about it. My sexuality and love life is such an insignificant part of who I am, and I really hate labels of any sort. I'm just Ricky. Don't get so stressed out and worked up over trying to pigeonhole me, because it really doesn't matter. I'm just me.

I will tell you this, though—I've never really been all that interested in having a relationship with anyone, period. I like to be alone. It's easy for me to use my YouTube career as an excuse to not get involved with anyone because I don't want anything to distract me from it, but I also just simply don't crave a relationship or love. I have friends who are constantly trying to set me up with a friend of theirs, and I always tell them, "I really don't want to." And I mean it. I truly don't. It's hard to talk about because most people don't get it. They think it's weird, I guess because the evolution of the species dictates that every guy wants to put his wiener *somewhere*, regardless of whether it will make a baby.

I definitely get little crushes from time to time, but nothing more serious, and I sometimes wonder if I have a hormone imbalance. Like, honestly, I mean that. It sounds dramatic, but seriously, something is off. Even if I do have an actual imbalance, though, I don't really mind. I don't get upset or down or sad in any way about any of this. It feels insignificant and irrelevant to my life at this point in time. I'm the happiest I've ever been by far. I lead a really fulfilling life, and I have the most fun when I'm creating things. Who knows, all of that could change in a heartbeat if I meet The One. I do like the idea of maybe having a family someday, but it's more of an abstract concept than anything else. At least for now.

So that's the story of my (lack of a) love life. Not very exciting, I know, but it gives me a whole lot more time to work on things to make *you* happy, and that's what fulfills me at the moment.

CHALLENGE

#FIRSTKISSFORRICKY

I want to hear first-kiss stories! But I also don't want anyone who hasn't had their first kiss yet to feel left out, so here's the compromise—describe your ultimate, craziest dream scenario for a first kiss with a celebrity of your choice.

CHALLENGE

#ELEVATORSINGFORRICKY

Get into a crowded elevator
and start singing really loud as
soon as the doors close.

SOCIAL

Remember those iChat sleepovers I used to have in college with the future O2L boys and my other YouTube friends? There were a couple of others who would join us sometimes— Rebecca Black and Jenn McAllister, aka jennxpenn.

Weird coincidence: Jenn started her YouTube channel exactly one day before mine! I watched all of her videos, and she was watching mine, too. We attracted the same sort of audience, and it didn't take long for us to start messaging each other as mutual admirers. I think she's an incredible content creator and it was obvious she worked super hard at what she did—and she still does. I respect and admire her a lot, and it's really cool to have gotten to know her so well way back in the day.

I finally met Jenn in person for the first time at the same VidCon where I met the O2L boys. Not long after we all got home, she got hacked. Since I tend to stay up super late at night a lot, I was one of the first to notice when around 3:00 a.m. a suspicious video asking for money suddenly appeared on her channel. I tried reaching her but she didn't pick up the phone, so I got in touch with someone else I'd met at VidCon who I knew had her home number, so I called and woke her mom up. I apologized over and over but told her it was an emergency. Jenn obviously freaked out, as anyone would have in that situation, and I stayed on the phone with her for hours while she got in touch with YouTube headquarters and tried to figure out what to do. I think that night really cemented our friendship.

She ended up moving to L.A. a month after Connor and I did, and got an apartment about half a block away from us with fellow YouTuber Andrea Russett. We frequently had Fiesta Nights, where Jc would cook all of us Mexican food, and afterward we'd take long walks around the neighborhood or go to the nearby movie theater. One night Jenn and Andrea broke into our apartment and covered everything in Silly String! That was hilarious until it came time to clean it up, then it kind of sucked. I adore her, though, and whenever we do a collab viewers really seem to like it. She's definitely one of my favorite people to work with. Normally any video I post will inevitably get some haters, but not when we do stuff together. We have a really strong connection that I think shows through, and always have a ridiculous amount of fun together.

My friendship with Rebecca Black is the same, and I even have her to thank for my getting over my fear of going to parties! It wasn't intentional on her part. Rebecca was already really well known back when we first met. One day I happened to notice that she was following me on Twitter, so I reached out to thank her and tell her how much I liked her videos, and she wrote back the sweetest message about how she had been watching my videos for a while! Kian had started messaging her around the same time, so we both invited her to iChat with us and pretty soon it became a regular thing. We've been close ever since.

After I moved to L.A., her sweet sixteen popped my L.A. party cherry and made me no longer afraid to walk into a houseful of people and loud music.

A friend of hers threw the bash, and I showed up with the whole neighborhood gang—Jenn, Andrea, Kian, Jc, and Connor. I felt all of my usual nerves flare up as we got closer and heard music thumping inside. But when we opened the door I realized I recognized the faces in the crowd. It wasn't a bunch of strangers—it was a bunch of other YouTubers! These were people I talked to online anyway.

I ended up having a great time. It wasn't even a particularly wild and crazy party, just a group of friends from the internet hanging out and dancing and talking. It was more than I'd ever experienced, though, and from then on I was never scared to go to parties.

I just wish I could remember if it had happened on a Friday.

CHALLENGE

#FIESTAFORRICKY

Host your own **Fiesta Night** for your
friends and/or family, with tons of
delicious Mexican food! *Olé!*

CHALLENGE

#COPYCATFORRICKY

Reenact one of my comedy
skit videos, line for line.

RANDOM

Hey, Disney Channel! You should call me, because I've got a brilliant idea for a new cartoon series. I've already got tons of episodes mapped out, in the form of a comic series I wrote and drew when I was seven years old. It's called *The Dream Team*!

The pitch:

> Five monsters that were created to wreak havoc on the world somehow get magically turned into good guys, build a secret lair inside a tree, and fight a rotating cast of baddies.

The characters:

> One is a giant head with a huge nose. This guy gets around thanks to a pair of hands that float beneath him and carry him wherever he wants to go. His power is SUPER STRENGTH! Next up is another floating head, but this one is a vampire with bat wings where his ears should be so he can fly. Third, we have a half circle with a cute face and nubby little legs, and he flies everywhere on a piece of electricity-infused scrap metal and tosses little bombs down to destroy bad guys. And we can't forget about the team member who is nothing but a big

squiggle with eyes! Mostly because I *did* forget what the fifth character I invented was.

I also created a series called *Penguinville*, which was all about a town where penguins lived as if they were humans, but this might be more of a niche market. The penguins all have hair and wear little bow ties, and their lives aren't quite as adventurous as the superheroes', but there's definitely penguin drama.

So, Disney, what do you think? Why don't you have your people call my people? I've got a really great feeling about this.

CHALLENGE

#CARTOONFORRICKY

Create your own cartoon superhero with
his/her/its own special set of powers.

CHAPTER 6

OBSTACLES

CHALLENGE

#LOVELISTFORRICKY

Make a list of everything you love about
a friend, family member, teacher—anyone
really—and randomly give it to that person.

MUSIC

As Taylor Swift has taught us, haters gonna hate. Sadly it's a fact of life, part of pretty much everyone's everyday existence. You'd think I'd be used to it by now, but I'm not. So why do I still let haters get to me sometimes?

I think it's because the most common kind of hate I get from strangers is about my music. When someone says something nasty about me in a challenge video, it's usually about my clothes, my hair, the way I talk, or some other irrelevant detail I never would have even noticed if they hadn't pointed it out. They'll find one little thing to nitpick about, and I can brush that off. Hands down, though, out of all the kinds of creative content I put out, the music is the most harshly judged, probably because it's such an emotionally vulnerable medium. Think about it—if you're acting, you're expressing emotions through words and expressions. With music, you're using those tools to do the same thing while also making your voice sound melodic and pleasing to listen to. Add dancing to the mix, and believe me, it ain't easy.

But I love making music so much because it's been such a huge part of my whole life. From dancing to Nicki Minaj while I'm cleaning to lip-syncing Aaron Carter songs in the car, all the way to making my own music, it shares an equal love in my heart with making YouTube videos. I'm not going to let anyone stop me from pursuing this dream. I make a big deal out of always saying that the haters don't have any power, but like I said, in real life they do get to me sometimes, especially if I'm already having a rough day.

There's a recurring pattern to how haters infiltrate my life. I'll post a new music video, and for the first few days I receive a flood of admiration and love from my supporters. Reading all of those sweet messages is like a natural high, an endorphin rush. Then, after about forty-eight hours, the vultures descend with their rude opinions and cruel observations and I'll come crashing down. What makes it worse is that a lot of the times a nasty comment will get bumped to the top of the comments section because of the number of replies it has gotten. (Fortunately, those replies tend to be people defending me, but they're hidden from view unless you click on them. The original comment is what stays front and center.)

I truly don't understand it. Why do people love to hate on performers when all we're doing is trying to put some fun out into the world? It's perfectly normal to not like *everything* out there—I certainly don't get down with every single music video I see or song I hear—but out of respect I would never publicly tear the performer down. Maybe haters secretly have ambitions of their own and are too nervous to put themselves out there because of a fear of failure.

Forget that, though! I work hard at what I do and don't need the burden of someone else's negativity. It would be one thing if someone just handed me a song and told me to go record it for money. But I either write or cowrite all my own stuff, I produce the videos and hire everyone involved myself. At the end of the day the final product rests on my shoulders, and I always stand by my releases. I'm proud of the stuff I create. I have a true passion for music, and no one should ever tell another person to stop doing something he or she loves, even if it's something they don't personally like. If people are doing something they love that isn't harming anyone else, then that should be encouraged and glorified, not torn down. If you don't like something, simply don't pay attention to it. Watching a video or listening to a song is a *choice*, and if you don't like what you see or hear then just move on. I don't understand why people waste time and energy trying to bring down the things they don't like. Literally, just get on with your life. It's much easier and much healthier. They say that success is in the eye of the beholder, and to me, success is being happy and doing what I love and that's what I'm doing.

I once watched an interview with the actress Gabourey Sidibe, and she said a really established movie star once told her, "Oh, honey, you should really quit the business. It's so image-conscious."

WHAT!? Look at Gabourey now! She's got an Academy Award nomination and currently stars on a hit TV show! She's so inspiring to me. I only get haters talking smack online in a comments section, but she had one of her heroes fat shame her to her face and Gabourey still marched on to become a major star. I wonder how that other actress (whom, incidentally, I haven't seen in anything for years) feels now. I hope she learned to stop judging people.

Thinking about that story manages to calm me down when I'm upset about haters. Another thing that I do to feel better is watch some of my favorite artists' music videos. You know why? Because people hate on them, too! I'm not saying that I specifically go *looking* for hate brought upon other people, but when I happen to see that even an incredible artist like Beyoncé gets negative comments, it reminds me that literally everyone gets hate. Not that I'm comparing myself to Beyoncé, but seeing that her amazing "7/11" video racked up over 180,000 dislikes on YouTube makes me realize I'm not alone. Beyoncé haters put everything in context—even the greats can't please everyone.

A lot of YouTubers, myself included, can often put on a show about not letting haters bother them. Trust me, we all have our days here and there where it can get to us. Everyone is insecure to some degree. It's unrealistic to expect people to ignore haters just because we tell them to. Unless you're a completely self-confident person, which is rare, that kind of healthy ego boosting takes work. My advice is to start inward. This sounds cheesy, but try looking in a mirror and telling yourself that you're awesome. If you don't believe it, do it again the next day, and the next. You can always look for love and support from your family and friends, but if you don't believe in yourself, then why should anyone else? I think that's how Gabourey was able to rise above everything she faced in Hollywood. As messed-up as it was for another actress to tell her to quit acting, the woman was right about one thing—the entertainment business *is* too image-conscious. But Gabourey believed in herself and didn't let that stop her.

If someone hates on something you've done creatively, I think it's probably healthier to get angry than to get sad about it. Because anger, as long as it doesn't get the best of you and is turned into good energy, can be a pretty good motivator. Try to harness those feelings to push you even further out of your own comfort zone. Take *more* risks. Remember: There's no better revenge than success.

CHALLENGE

#SPREADLOVEFORRICKY

Send a tweet to someone you admire
(celebrity, teacher, friend, Supreme
Court judge, etc.) and tell that person
why you think he or she is awesome.

CHALLENGE

#DRAWRICKYFORRICKY

Draw or paint a picture of me and post it!

SELF-EMPOWERMENT

ike every other human being on this planet, I have skin that secretes natural oils. Except I think God decided to give me a little extra. And when I have hot, bright lights shining in my face all day when I'm shooting a video, my face turns into an industrial fryer. Luckily, there's a solution for that. Face powder! Otherwise known as makeup. Unfortunately, there are a lot of ignorant people out there who think guys shouldn't wear makeup.

It's not like I wear lipstick, eye shadow, and mascara on top of it, but you know what? Even if I did, WHO CARES? People, we are living in 2016, and there is no place left in this world for the idea that gender should dictate what someone can or can't do. Gender roles are set by society, and as a society, we need to get over them. The concept that boys can't play with dolls and girls shouldn't get down and dirty building a tree house is so outdated, and yet somehow people still believe the myth.

When I was a little kid I was obsessed with the cartoon *Animaniacs*. Of the three main characters, the female, Dot, was hands down my favorite. She was cute and sassy and made me laugh more than any other creature on the show. One day my mom took me to a Toys "R" Us and I went off in search of a Dot stuffed animal. I found the *Animaniacs* toys in an aisle marked "Boys," but there were no Dots to be found. On a hunch, I walked over to the girls' section and sure enough saw a big pile of Dot stuffed animals at the far end of an aisle. I got about three steps closer when a store worker stepped up and said, "Excuse me, this is the little girls' section. The boy toys are over there." I slunk away, humiliated. I felt like I had done something horribly wrong, but at the same time I knew in my heart that there was *nothing* wrong with my wanting a Dot doll. It was a toy that would have made me happy, end of story. It had nothing to do with my gender.

There have definitely been some positive changes since then. Target has stopped labeling toys as being made for boys or girls, but that's just one small step. We've still got a long way to go. I know this firsthand because of nasty commenters. Instead of focusing on a video I've just made for them, some people only pay attention to the fact that they can tell I'm wearing makeup. It's like they seek it out on my face or something. Trust me, people, it's for your benefit, not mine. If I didn't use makeup, I'd look like the next BP oil spill disaster, and those are never fun to look at. When I don't wear makeup in videos people comment on my oily face, and then when I do wear makeup people comment on that. So I just end up doing what makes me feel the most confident with myself on any given day. Sometimes I don't need it at all!

The powder also helps to disguise the fact that my face turns red and blotchy when I feel any kind of heightened emotion. I'm very insecure about it, but I'm not ashamed of it or anything. I just know that it would be a distraction from whatever was happening in the video, and the action is what I want people to focus on.

Aside from stopping me from getting a toy I wanted back in 1997, another big problem with gender roles is that a lot of people confuse them with sexuality. Like, if a girl wants to play football then she must be a lesbian. Wrong wrong wrong. You should never assume you know what someone's sexuality is. You wait for them to tell you themselves. It's ignorant and uncalled for to assume you know someone's sexuality simply based on something they're interested in.

If someone tells you that you can't do something just because you're a boy or a girl, ignore that person. Know that you are smarter than that. No one should ever stop you from doing what you want based on some lame concept of what's considered "normal." Every time you shatter someone's assumption about gender roles, we are that much closer to abolishing them.

CHALLENGE

#MAKEUPFORRICKY

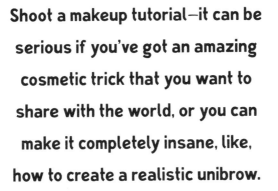

Shoot a makeup tutorial—it can be
serious if you've got an amazing
cosmetic trick that you want to
share with the world, or you can
make it completely insane, like,
how to create a realistic unibrow.

CHALLENGE

#CELEBMAKEOVERFORRICKY

Either give or receive a celebrity
makeover, where one of you dresses
the other up like a famous person.

SOCIAL

love being part of the Miranda Sings expanded-family universe so much. Even though our "relationship" is nothing more than the delusional fabrication of a psycho soprano, being one of her (many) boyfriends is an honor I don't take lightly. I've even gotten the chance to perform that role live at one of her shows, when she called me out of the audience to participate in a Q&A session on how to behave in a movie theater on a first date.

One day I drove over to Colleen's house to shoot a video, but something prevented us from getting started right away. I found her pacing furiously up and down her lawn, totally freaking out. I jumped out of my car, thinking she'd been robbed.

"'What's wrong?" I asked, running up to her.

"Oh, my god, Ricky, LOOK!"

She pointed to the window next to her front door but I didn't see anything.

"It's a bat!" she screamed.

"Where?"

She dragged me closer to the front of the house, where I finally noticed the leathery little guy curled up in a corner of the sill.

"I was watching TV and it just flew out from behind the screen, out of nowhere!"

The image kind of cracked me up but she was so bugged

out that I figured it wasn't a good idea to laugh. Her husband wasn't home and she had no idea how to get rid of it. "You have to help me," she begged.

Bats aren't my favorite animals in the world either. We decided it was a bad idea to try to walk in the front door, since it was sitting right next to it, so we crept around to the back of the house and entered from there. We tiptoed through the kitchen and into the living room, where we saw it quivering in the same spot we'd seen from outside. It seemed to want to get out of the house as much as we wanted it to leave.

"I think it needs more convincing," I said. "What do you have that we can throw at it?"

"You can't hurt it!" Colleen wailed. "That's cruel!"

"No, I mean, not at it, but *near* it. Maybe if we can startle it, it will start flying around and realize the door is open."

"But what if it starts flying around and comes right at us instead?" she asked.

"Do you have a better idea?"

She shrugged and we looked around for soft things to toss that wouldn't damage the bat or her walls. Once we had collected a bunch of things like small pillows and wooden spoons from the kitchen, we crouched down and took turns lobbing them to the left of the bat. At first it just looked at us, annoyed, but then it started to fidget, and every time it made a sudden motion we'd both yelp.

I can't remember what object we tossed that finally made it get off its butt and start to fly around, but as soon as it launched we both started screaming our heads off. If we had been smart we would have charged toward it to try to herd it outside, but instead we covered our heads with our hands and dropped them between our knees. "Don't let it get in my hair!" she screamed.

It finally calmed down, and I started to stealthily walk toward the door so I could open it and let the little guy out. But suddenly it leaped back up and flew right at us, so we started screaming and booked it out into the backyard.

Fortunately, her husband, Josh, was just pulling into the driveway, and we hid behind him as he casually managed to simply nudge the bat out the front door.

I felt kind of dumb, standing there surrounded by an arsenal of harmless weapons littering the floor, but the look of relief on Colleen's face was priceless.

"Come on," I said, helping her up from the floor. "We've got a video to film."

CHALLENGE

#MIRANDASCREAMSFORRICKY

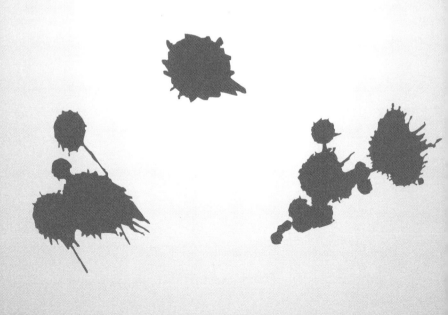

Tweet pictures of scary-looking
bats to Miranda Sings! (Sorry
in advance, Miranda!)

#YOGAFORRICKY

Invent the most insane yoga
position imaginable.

FAMILY

Have you ever watched one of devinsupertramp's videos? Basically he films friends doing crazy extreme sports stunts that look more like special effects than anything a human being would actually be able to do. He was looking for some YouTubers to collaborate with and reached out to me, Jenn, and Jack Baran to see if we wanted to shoot some stunts with him. Heck yeah!

We *really* should have paid closer attention to the fine print in our itinerary. We knew that Devin travels all over the globe for his videos, and we were all so busy that when we heard we were going to Utah, it didn't exactly ring any alarms in our heads. Salt Lake City is less than two hours away from L.A. by plane. NBD, and besides, Jordan, our talent manager at the time, was coming along with us.

When we landed, we discovered that we then had to drive SIX HOURS to get to a lake where we needed to be! We were annoyed, but knew it was totally our own fault for not asking for more specific details about the trip, so we sucked it up and Jordan rented a car. The drive took us through these really intense mountain ranges, and at first it felt like an exciting adventure, but when we hit the desert and the road just stretched on and on and on it got boring fast.

We finally arrived at the lake and it was stunning—it looked like a massively long blue snake that wound through sand-colored cliffs for 186 MILES.

A man in a speedboat was waiting for us at a dock when we parked. We were too exhausted from the drive to make much conversation and as soon as we pulled away from the shore he told us it would be *another* hour before we reached the house-boat (that's how huge this lake is).

At that point we felt too beaten down to even react. We took in the view and checked our phones and about halfway into the trip the man turned around from the wheel and said, "Better send your last texts. In about five minutes you won't have cell service for the next three days. Isn't it nice to get away from it all?"

We immediately began to panic.

I can't stand to be offline. It makes me super anxious to an uncomfortable extent. The internet is my entire career! I have obligations on a daily basis that are online and require internet access. I'm constantly worried when I get disconnected that there will be an emergency I need to know about or take care of. Basically, I don't like being completely cut off from every-thing when my whole professional life revolves around being online.

It was much worse for Jenn and Jack that time, though. They both had videos they needed to finish editing for brand deals that were due in forty-eight hours! They'd brought their laptops, thinking they could finish cutting what they needed and then just email them to their sponsors. There was no turn-ing back, though, and they weren't even able to fire off texts to their managers to tell them they were about to lose service be-fore we went out of range. I don't think any of us quite believed that there would be *no* way to get online. We figured there had to be Wi-Fi on the boat or a mobile hotspot or at least that we'd be able to easily reach the shore and find service there somewhere. I tried to push the thought of something terrible happening to my mom and my family not being able to reach me out of my head, and we all decided that we just needed to try to make the most of where we were and have fun.

We finally arrived at the boat and it was huge—there were three levels, and it was anchored in a cove next to a massive cliff that went up and up and up. It felt like we were on Mars, if Mars had water. And boats.

There were tons of people lounging around and leaping into the water. Music was blaring and everyone was laughing, and there was a huge inflatable thing attached to the back and floating on the surface of the lake, sort of like a bouncy castle but shaped like a huge tube. Everyone called it The Blob.

It turned out that the guy who'd driven us also owned the houseboat, and he started going through a giant list of rules about everything that we could and couldn't touch, and how to properly flush the toilets, and then told us there were no beds left so we would literally have to sleep on the floor outside. That last part was actually kind of cool. We could see a million stars all the way out there in the middle of nowhere. The captain was starting to give off a really bad vibe, though, like he was seriously regretting renting his boat out to Devin and his giant crew.

We woke up early the next morning and got to work shooting. The Blob turned out to be a human-projectile launcher. I would sit at one end of it, and someone else would stand at the top of the boat and jump down on the other end, which would cause me to go flying fifty feet into the air and then splash down into the water. We got to fly around the cove in water-powered jet packs, and it was all so much fun that we forgot about the rest of the world. At the end of the day Jenn and Jack started to really freak out about not being able to reach their managers to explain why their videos were delayed. We all hated the idea of missing a deadline—we knew how lucky we were to have internet careers in the first place and didn't want to do anything that might hurt them. It's bad enough to miss a deadline, but it's even worse when you can't send any messages to explain the situation. Their managers were totally in the dark about what was happening and had no way to reach them.

Devin had gotten so many shots of us that day that we couldn't really understand why they needed us to stay for two more days. We talked to him and Jordan and asked if we could leave early and they both totally understood. It's not like we were even getting paid to be there, so it wouldn't hurt anyone if we ditched. Jordan said he'd ask the captain to drive us back to our car the next morning, and we went to sleep that night totally relieved.

At dawn, the captain shot us down.

"I'm getting ready to sell that speedboat," he said. "I can't just go adding tons more miles onto it, and that would be an extra two-hour round-trip for me. Not gonna happen."

Jordan and Devin were both really embarrassed and apologetic, and we were horrified. We were trapped in the middle of a lake with no way of getting out! It wasn't even like we could have swum to shore and hitchhiked, because the boat was surrounded by cliffs!

We could see a few more houseboats bobbing in the water in the distance, and as a total joke I said, "We should go see if we have any viewers on one of those, maybe they'll drive us back."

Before I knew it Jordan had jumped on a jet ski like some sort of superhero and ridden off to find out.

He struck gold on the first try. There were some kids on board who knew us! Jordan invited them over to our boat and we took photos with them, and then asked if we could pay their parents to drive us back to shore. They did! Devin was relieved for us, and I could tell he felt awful about what a jerk the captain was being.

When we finally got back to the rental car we drove to a small town and stopped at a motel with Wi-Fi, where Jenn and Jack were able to spend the evening handling their videos. All's well that ends well, I guess, except for one thing—we were cut from the final video!

CHALLENGE

#WATERSPORTSFORRICKY

Try a water stunt that you've never done—think jet skis, surfing, paddle boarding, high diving, even plain old body surfing if you've never had the pleasure.

CHALLENGE

#LYRICCONVOFORRICKY

Try to keep up a conversation with a
friend in which each of you can only
use famous song lyrics and film it.

HEALTH

Confession: I'm jealous of a lot of my friends. The ones who can eat whatever junk food they want and never work out and somehow still look amazing. They won the genetic lottery (go buy my song "Lottery" on iTunes!), something I definitely did not when it comes to trying to stay jacked. If I was naturally fit and had a fast metabolism, I'd probably look like Arnold Schwarzenegger circa the first *Terminator* with how much I work out. As it is, if I don't work out for a week or two I quickly lose any physique I've gained. It's the reason I'm so hard-core about going to the gym. I can see my muscles deflate overnight if I don't keep at it.

I know this might come across as vain, but that's not it at all. In fact, it's the total opposite. It has everything to do with my insecurity over cultural body expectations. Women have had to deal with unrealistic standards for decades, and I think it's gotten pretty bad for guys, too. I can't turn around without seeing another photo of a ripped, shirtless man promising me that my life would be perfect if I could just have a body like his. It makes me self-conscious and uncomfortable, and I end up thinking that the only way to make those feelings go away is to work out harder, eat even healthier.

Keeping the motivation up gets tiring, and a lot of times I have to force myself to exercise after a long day. I know that working out and eating healthy is only a good thing, so a lot of times when I'm trying to get the energy up to do it I try to only focus on that aspect, instead of anyone else's idea of what I should look like. A person's *reasons* for working out and eating right should be as healthy as the results that come from doing those things.

CHALLENGE

#VEGANFORRICKY

Make a vegan dinner, post a picture, and describe how it tasted (I promise I won't be offended if you hate it). If you're already a vegan, share a pic of your favorite vegan meal and use #KISSMEIMVEGAN instead!

CHALLENGE

#UNDERWATERFORRICKY

Using a waterproof camera, take
an underwater selfie—it can be
in a pool, a lake, the ocean, a
bathtub, the kitchen sink, wherever
you want. Just don't drown.

RANDOM

You know how when you were little and still figuring out how the world works the tiniest little thing could set you off on a major tantrum? Like, a Cheerio could fall off your spoon and next thing you know you're facedown on the ground howling at the unfairness of the universe? No big deal, it's a normal part of the growing experience. I hope you had smart parents like I did. They didn't indulge that sort of behavior. They taught me when it was acceptable to get angry and try to overcome whatever it was that was bothering me, and when I just needed to accept a situation for what it was. That's why I was able to stay so calm and rational when, in kindergarten, a kid split my head open so wide that I still have a huge scar on my forehead today.

Here's how it went down: Every day after recess, a different student would get chosen as the Line Leader. The responsibilities included moving to the front of the line and holding the door to the school open so the rest of the class could file back inside. That's it. My class had a game that we'd always play, in which every time you passed the Line Leader, you had to tag him or her, and the Line Leader had to tag the person back before he or she got inside the door. Nothing major, just a simple tap on the shoulder. Thrilling, right?

So one day it's my turn as Line Leader, and we're tap, tap, tapping away when this kid named Barry comes by and reaches out to get my shoulder. Only he put a little more momentum into it than necessary, and I went flying headfirst into the razor-sharp corner of the industrial-grade door latch.

I'm not exaggerating when I say blood exploded everywhere. It looked like Freddy Krueger had just taken a swipe at my face, and I can still feel that hot liquid running into my eyes and burning them. But I stayed strangely calm. I listened to all the kids around me screaming and watched my teacher's face contort in shock, as if in slow motion. Her mouth became a perfect circle and her eyes bulged out of her head like a cartoon. But nothing beat the look on Barry's face. He was HORRIFIED. I knew he hadn't meant to hurt me. We were friendly with each other. It was just another playground game gone hideously wrong.

It didn't hurt, and now that I think about it I was probably in shock. The entire front of my shirt was drenched red and everyone still had no idea what to do. Thank God my sister Tara happened to be walking down the hallway and saw what was happening. She snapped into action, scooped me up, and rushed me to the nurse's office.

You know things aren't going well when even the school nurse looks like she's going to faint after getting a glimpse of your face.

I remember being wrapped up in a blanket and the nurse trying to wipe away the blood, but it had no intention of slowing down. Next thing I knew my mom was there, bundling me into her car and driving me to the emergency room. Good thing, too, because it turned out that I needed thirty-eight stitches.

Thus ended the era of Line Leader. The school got a big ol' doorstop to use instead.

When I returned to school, Barry felt very guilty. He kept apologizing over and over and I had to keep telling him it was no big deal. Because it wasn't. Sure, the doctor told me that due to the size and depth of the cut I'd have a scar for the rest of my life, but now I love it. It's kind of cool, and just another example of an imperfection that makes me unique. (Weirdly, Connor has a scar in almost the exact same place!) More important, I knew that what had happened was an accident. There was no point in getting mad. What was done was done and there was no malice behind the incident.

There are some parents out there who probably would have tried to sue the school for what happened, and *that's* what gets me mad. Everyone makes dumb mistakes sometimes, and the idea of punishing someone for that is absurd. It's called life. Stuff happens!

CHALLENGE

#TRAUMADRAMAFORRICKY

Tell the story of your most embarrassing moment or craziest injury.

CHAPTER 7

GRATEFUL

CHALLENGE

#ICEBATHFORRICKY

Do the ice bath challenge with a friend—
see who can stay in a tub full of ice the
longest. (Be safe and smart, though!)

FAMILY

As I've mentioned, I was an almost embarrassingly well-behaved kid growing up. I never got in trouble, and I didn't drink, smoke, or cuss. I'd like to say I was naturally born a good person, but I know that I have my parents to thank for how I turned out. They were strict, but not too strict. They instilled a moral code in me from as early as I can remember and taught me the difference between right and wrong. I remember realizing from a very early age that I should always treat people the same way I wanted to be treated, and that came directly from them.

That's not to say I didn't act out sometimes. I could be a typical bratty little brother to Tara. We shared a bathroom and I used to go through all of her hair products and throw them around or hide them in the dirty laundry. I'd get my Game Boy taken away for a day and that would be the end of it. There were never any screaming matches or slamming doors. On rare occasions I'd act out by saying I didn't feel like doing my homework. No kid wants to do homework, but I did want to do well in school, so all it took was the threat of being grounded to snap me back into line.

I know, I know. I sound like the most boring kid on earth. No one is ever going to accuse me of being the face of youth gone wild. I feel like kids and teenagers who do go through a rebellious period are usually just looking for answers about their place in the world, and my parents never gave me any reason to doubt mine. I felt safe and was well taken care of.

All that being said, I did start to shut them out a little bit around my junior year of high school. When I was younger and got made fun of for the way I talked, I'd always tell them about it and look to them for comfort, but once I became a teenager I relied on my friends for that kind of support. I became more reserved and private at home. I didn't ice my folks out completely or anything, but like any normal teenager, I was much more comfortable talking about personal things like my insecurities with my friends.

Moving away to college forced me to reconnect. I was so lonely and homesick that I tore down the wall I'd built up around them. (Fine, it was more like a white picket fence.) I called them a lot to moan about how unhappy I was, but they didn't indulge my complaints. I know that if I had been seriously depressed they would have pulled me out of college, but I think they could tell I was more dissatisfied than anything else. So they told me to just buckle down, get back to work, and stick it out.

I was a little bit worried when I decided to switch my major to film from pharmacy. I thought my dad might be disappointed that I was dropping out of the field he worked in. Nope. He knew how much I loved making videos so he understood that choosing film as my new major was a natural progression for my life.

Today, I'm just as close to my parents as ever, but I know how easy it is to take them for granted. I get swept up in daily life and I'll forget to call one of them back and suddenly realize a week has gone by and I haven't spoken to either of them. That scares me. Not to sound morbid, but I would never forgive my-self if there were some sort of accident and my last words ever to them were, "Can't talk, gotta collab, byeeeee!"

Every day should be Father's Day and Mother's Day. And Stepparents' Day, or Legal Guardian's Day. When you're a teenager it's so easy to get swept up in hormones and drama and lash out at them. The next time you feel like taking your fury at the world out on your mom, take a deep breath and ask yourself if what you're about to say to her is something legiti-mately directed at your relationship with her, or if you're just using her as a punching bag. In the heat of the moment it can be hard to tell the difference.

CHALLENGE

#PARENTPRESENTFORRICKY

There's an episode of *Keeping Up with the Kardashians* where the kids put together a whole music video for Kris on her birthday to show their love. In that spirit I want you to do some

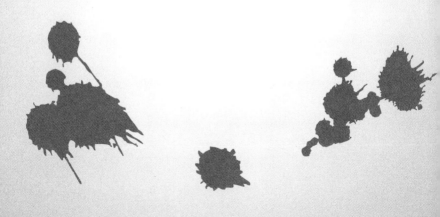

sort of creative project for your own mom/dad/guardian, to show your appreciation for all they do. It can be a poster, a video message, a handpicked bouquet, whatever you want.

CHALLENGE

#DRIVETHRUFORRICKY

Get a friend to film you ordering something that's not on the menu at a fast-food drive-thru, and insist that they do have it.

MUSIC

After my EP came out and I decided I wanted to keep on recording music, Trevor Moran hooked me up with a producer he'd worked with before named Bobby J Frausto. I'm eternally grateful and bow down to you, Trevor, for introducing us.

I'd already recorded a few songs with one production team but I like mixing things up, and from the first day that I started recording with Bobby J, I knew he was the one I wanted to stick with.

For starters, he helped me so much with my voice. He worked with me until we found a tone and range that really suit me. Up until that point I was still experimenting with my voice and trying to find out what my vocal niche was. Even though I'd been singing for two years I could still get really nervous about it, and he was the first producer I'd collaborated with who took the time to sit down and really listen to what works best for me in terms of singing. Not that I'm saying my other producers weren't great, too, it's just that Bobby J really took me under his wing to help me define my sound.

His studio is in his house, which is a two-hour drive from Los Angeles, almost all the way to San Diego. Every trip was worth it. For one thing, I had plenty of time to warm up my voice each time I went because I'd sing in the car! His place is kind of like a mini mansion that he lives in with his business partner, Steve (who is also an incredible producer and sound engineer and worked on some of my songs with Bobby). Their place is out in the middle of nowhere so everything is very quiet and serene, with views of rolling hills that seem to go on forever. When we first started working together, we'd spend whole days just hanging out, writing lyrics, and coming up with new sounds. Some days we wouldn't even do that much—we'd just brainstorm concepts. I bonded and meshed so well with him. I never felt like I was working; it was always fun.

Once we got down to actually recording, he wouldn't just stick me in the recording booth and let me go at it. We'd sit down and practice each song, and he'd give me all sorts of advice about the best way to deliver certain words or notes. Then we'd do a demo version and listen to it together, picking out all the places that could use improvement or minor tweaking. By the time Bobby J and I finally got around to actually recording, the song would go so smoothly because we'd put in so much prep work beforehand. It was the same level of dedication that I always got from my music video director Andrew Vallentine.

Originally I thought I was just recording another EP, but Bobby J and I worked so well and so long together that before I knew it I had eight songs written. So I decided to come up with two more and release a full album.

When we were working on the last song, "Problematic," Bobby J suddenly had the brilliant idea that it should have a rap feature. I was immediately into it. He has worked with major people like Ne-Yo, Wiz Khalifa, and Snoop Dogg, and he thought Snoop would be perfect for the job.

Bobby J reached out to Snoop and his team, and I couldn't

believe it when he agreed to do it! He said that he loved the song and was really into YouTube, so it was a perfect fit. I got to meet him on the night we went to his studio to record his part, and he was so humble and nice. When we shot the video not long after, he showed up with a whole crew, but all of them were super chill, too. Since he's a big celeb he totally could have acted like a diva on set, but nothing could be further from the truth. He was a total professional and sweet. We shot his bit in Crenshaw outside the Uneek Socks shop. (He has a really cool line with them and you should check them out!)

When I released my first EP, things that were out of my control kept setting our deadline further and further back, and eventually I got so tired of waiting that I rushed through it a little too much just to get the music out. With this album, I know I've taken the time to give each song the love that it deserves. I started making my song "Gold" all the way back in April 2015 and didn't wrap that track up until November! I think it's really important to give any creative project you take on room to breathe. If you feel rushed, your brain is going to seize up and panic and you won't get your best work done. (Unless you're one of those people who thrive under pressure and deadlines. If that's your jam, then by all means, go ahead and slack off!)

For me, though, I know how lucky I am to have the freedom to take my time to do a project the way I want it to be done, and I'm seriously blessed to be surrounded by so many creative people who have helped me achieve my goals.

If you have some sort of artistic project that you're working on, don't ever be afraid to ask for help with it if you get stuck on something. Sometimes even just talking out loud about a problem you're having will cause a brilliant solution to pop into your head. If there are people you admire in your school and you think they could teach you a thing or two about acting or photography or film or whatever, don't be afraid to approach them and ask for advice. Chances are they will be flattered—everyone likes to be told they're good at something. If you're into music as much as I am and want to record a song, you don't even need to search out a mentor. All you have to do is download some music production software like GarageBand or Stagelight and produce it yourself! It's easier than ever these days to mix your own music. In fact, the same goes for all the mediums I just listed above. There's a program for almost any creative project that will answer many questions and teach you new things.

CHALLENGE

#WRITEASONGFORRICKY

Write a song! It can be serious or silly, long or short, rhyme or not, whatever you want. (See what I did there?) If you're a singer, record yourself singing it. If you're not or are just feeling shy, then either get a friend to, or simply read the lyrics out loud.

CHALLENGE

#STOPMOTIONFORRICKY

I used to love making stop-motion
videos when I was just starting out on
YouTube. Make one of your own, using
either your body or objects or both!

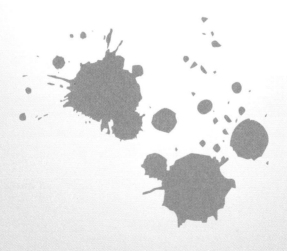

HEALTH

When I used to play tennis, I had a whole team and a coach who motivated me to work out. Once I moved to L.A., I was pretty much on my own at the gym. I knew that there were things I wanted to change and learn about my body, so once I was settled in at the O2L house in Encino, I hired my very first personal trainer.

His name was Sammy, and he worked at the gym I belonged to, L.A. Fitness. I mean it in the nicest way possible when I say that Sammy is a total ball buster. His motivation method was to be . . . how do I say this. Not quite *mean*, but almost. Let's go with very tough, but in a good way. He pushed me in a way that I needed to be pushed at a time when I was really into making some big changes to my body in terms of gaining muscle. He taught me about endurance and testing my limits, but not to the point where I might hurt myself. He could always tell when I hit my wall and would pull back.

If you want to get a good sense of just how terrifying, I mean, *motivating*, Sammy can be, check out a video on Kian and Jc's channel called "House Robbery Prank." They got Sammy to dress up all in black and cover his face with a bandana and a hoodie and pretend to be a house invader. I thought we were all about to be murdered, although now I understand why the guy kept screaming "Turn around!" every time I tried to crane my neck. Sammy didn't want me to get a look at him and figure the whole thing out. If you watch it until the end after the prank is revealed, you can also get a glimpse of Sammy's arms. Dude is a beast, and you'll be able to tell why I knew as soon as I met him that he was the right guy to whip me into shape.

After we moved to the Hollywood Hills, Encino was too far away for me to drive and meet with Sammy every day. I joined a 24-Hour Fitness closer to our new place, so I asked for one of their in-house guys and that's how I met Matt.

Matt's specialty was food. He's the one who taught me how important nutrition is to a workout. He told me what I should or shouldn't eat before running or lifting in order to get the maximum benefit from our bodywork. He's the one who taught me the trick about how if you're going to eat carbs you should do it in the morning so you have the rest of the day to burn them off. He was always going on about how bad preservatives are for your body. Initially I thought a lot of what he was telling me was common knowledge that I already understood from health class back in elementary school, but he always took the time to explain the reasons *why* a certain food was either good or bad for me, and how it could specifically affect my body or mood. It wasn't long before I realized that all of my eating habits had changed for the better, and it was all because of his influence. I had more energy all of the time, my skin had never looked better, and I found that I could work out for much longer than ever before. Because of Matt, my stamina went through the roof.

When I moved to Venice I once again lost the convenient proximity to my trainer. By that time, though, I felt comfortable enough to take everything Sammy and Matt had taught me and go it alone. I still saw Matt every now and then, but I missed having a regular partner. One year at Playlist Live I met a guy named Justin, who was roommates with Scott and Mitch from the a cappella group Pentatonix. (Scott and Mitch also have their own YouTube channel called Superfruit.)

Justin looked really good. He basically had the body I wanted, so I asked him for some fitness tips. It turned out that he lives kind of near me so we started hitting the gym together as workout buddies, and he ended up teaching me many little things I hadn't learned from the other guys about form. He explained all these techniques that were new to me, ones that target even the most random little muscle to help really build and sculpt definition. He showed me things I never would have thought of, and I've grown much stronger since I met him.

I'm so grateful to each of these guys. I'm happy with the way I look and I owe so much of it to them. All three are super fit, and each had his own individual ways of getting to that point. I got the best of all their combined ideas and have been able to create workouts that pull the maximum benefit from each of their strengths. They're like the Power Rangers if there were only three of them, and when you combine their powers, you get a Mega Ricky!

Ugh, that's a terrible metaphor. How about I leave it at this: I'm grateful to Sammy, Matt, and Justin because each showed me how to push myself and discover everything I'm capable of doing with my body. None of them ever held back with me, which is the sign of a great teacher. I only hope that I can inspire some people to live healthier and happier lives through fitness in the same way these guys inspired me.

CHALLENGE

#TRAINFORRICKY

Sharing is caring—reach out to someone in your life who really knows fitness and ask him or her to teach you something new about working out. It can be a friend, gym teacher, an actual trainer, anyone! The important thing is to not be scared to ask for advice.

CHALLENGE

#PLANKFORRICKY

Remember planking? Bring that back—it's great for your abs! Do it in a crazy place or a public spot.

RANDOM

Sometimes it's still hard for me to believe I have an album out. I put so much thought and effort into it, and I want to share a bit of that process with you. So here are the real meanings behind each of the songs, along with my favorite lyrics!

"Home Sweet Home"
This song is all about the feeling I get whenever I go back to my hometown. Walking down the streets and remembering who I used to be and how far I've come is so humbling. I made the lyrics broad enough though that I hope it will appeal to anyone who misses the good old days.
Favorite lines: "Looking out into the stars and moon, wishing now that I'll be coming home to you."

"Don't Want to Fall in Love"
Like I said earlier, I love being single. In the future, I might want to settle down and have a family, but right now I'm not looking for a relationship or love. If I find it, cool. But this is an anthem about being single and celebrating yourself.
Favorite lines: "Date you if I could, wishing that I would. Single is the way to go."

"Problematic"

I wanted to make a fun, sassy song—a different sort of clubby track about having a really fun night and not worrying about the world. Like causing a total ruckus, without getting *too* crazy.

Favorite lines: "Lookin' at ya in my ride, yeah you endorse it."

"Fight and Battle"

Most of the songs on *Gold* are pretty upbeat and carefree. This one is extra special to me because it's one of the most personal. I open up more than I ever have before, and talk about the insecurities I've had all my life and about all of the internal battles with myself trying to fight them off.

Favorite line: "Today I'm stronger from the pain of yesterday."

"Lottery"

The very first song I made for the album! It's about that first feeling you get when you realize you have a crush on someone, that beautiful and scary butterflies-in-your-stomach feeling.

Favorite lines: "Is this paradise? What Heaven feels like? Had you in my sights when you fell from the sky."

"Steal the Show," with Trevor Moran

We wrote this together, since any time we're together we try to grab all of the attention in the room! I think the video we shot for it gets the point across pretty well.

Favorite lines: "Everywhere they hearin' us and everywhere they feelin' us. Now let's go, now you know, this is how we steal the show."

"Gold"

After being bullied in high school for things like my speech impediment, it's still amazing to me that my life is and career are gold now, and this song celebrates overcoming those difficulties.

Favorite lines: "Now it's time to set myself free, letting go of it all to experience me."

"Got Your Back," with Shelby Waddell

There's nothing better than a best-friend anthem, and Shelby and I came up with this one together after writing down all of the stories and special memories we have about each other. We made sure that it's also a song for *anyone's* BFF!

Favorite lines: "Together through it all, no one can compete with that, just know I always got your back."

"Ordinary," acoustic version

Since "Ordinary" was my very first song, I wanted an opportunity to show my growth as a songwriter and vocalist. I stripped it way down and added a bridge to the lyrics, which it didn't have before.

Favorite lines: "I don't care if I stand out, it's what life is all about."

"Never Ending Runs," Cesar remix

I always felt like the original version of this song was missing something. Like, it kept building up, but never went anywhere. So I got my friend Cesar to remix it with an EDM drop. Fun fact: The guy who originally wrote this song is the same guy who did "Replay" for Zendaya.

Favorite lines: "We're here, we're free and we're young, living life our way."

CHALLENGE

#HAIKUFORRICKY

Write a haiku using only words
lifted from my favorite song lyrics!
Remember—a haiku is just three lines.
Five syllables in the first, seven in
the second, and five again in the last.
Here, I'll show you how easy it is!

Through it all stronger
Know what life is all about
Set myself free now

CHALLENGE

#SHIRTDESIGNFORRICKY

Make a shirt! You can use either a blank T-shirt and decorate and/or draw on it with fabric markers, or if you know how to sew, come up with something completely new!

SOCIAL

When I first started my YouTube channel in high school, my entire goal was to entertain and make people laugh. Nothing there has changed.

I didn't have a whole lot of self-confidence back then. It's not like I was a total loner—I definitely had several amazing friends whom I loved—but, aside from Shelby and Mason and my other close buddies, I didn't really like to be around people. Not because people annoyed me, but because I was always scared of saying or doing the wrong thing. My social anxiety was pretty much paralyzing, and sometimes I wonder how many opportunities I missed in life when I was younger because of that.

Since the very first day I started my channel, every single thumbs-up or sweet comment I've received has helped to raise me out of that place and to become a completely different person. I've become more confident, happier, and now have a much more positive outlook on life, all because of you! The people who watch my videos have changed my life in such a crazy deep, profound way that I feel like I could say "thank you" a trillion times and it would never be enough. You give me the motivation to keep going, the inspiration to come up with new ideas, and enough faith in myself to pull myself back up whenever something gets me down.

The best is when I get to meet you in person at events. Not

even because you're so nice to me (which you most definitely are), but more because I love seeing people make new friends when they've come together with a bunch of other people who have the same interests. It makes me feel so good to see you all out there having fun with each other, able to connect with strangers in a way I never could have when I was younger.

My favorite comments that I get on my videos aren't the ones that compliment me, they're the ones in which people write that they were having a terrible day and I was able to cheer them up and bring them out of that headspace. With all that you do for me emotionally, I'm so happy I can give even that much back. I would be nowhere in life without you.

CHALLENGE

#CHEERUPFORRICKY

Post your favorite thing that you
do to make yourself feel better
if you're having a terrible day.
(Besides watch my videos! ☺)

CHALLENGE

#SHORTFILMFORRICKY

Make a short movie that's less than ten minutes long. It's got to have a plot with a clear beginning, middle, and end. Don't sweat the special effects, unless you want to!

SELF-EMPOWERMENT

Demi Lovato is a huge inspiration to me. She is the living embodiment of perseverance and true talent. The fact that she went into recovery at such a young age and has managed to stick with it without crashing means she must have an iron spirit. In a way I feel like I've grown up alongside her. Actually, I have. We're the same age, and I've charted her personal growth along with my own every step of the way, ever since her days on *As the Bell Rings* and *Sonny with a Chance*.

Her song "Really Don't Care" has always meant so much to me. I know it's technically about the end of a relationship, but the chorus is just so, I don't know, *universal* somehow. To be able to say that you don't care about something that has hurt you, be it a person or just a life moment that's knocked you down a peg, and to actually truly *mean* those words, is such a freeing experience. Chanting "I really don't care" along with her is an anthem to everyone and anything that has ever hurt you. It gives you your power back.

By the summer of 2014 I was still riding high on releasing the video for "Ordinary." It was getting tons of attention and support, but as always, there were haters. People telling me I had no business trying to be a singer, and that I should stick to my regular videos. Even worse were the people who made fun of my speech impediment. Who even are these people? Was I suddenly in middle school again?

But I didn't care. I was suddenly in a place in my life where I loved being myself—something I learned from Demi—and I was feeling more self-confident than ever before. I genuinely didn't care what people thought of how I looked or acted. It was sort of an epiphany, because even though I'd had so much fun shooting "Ordinary," and had felt so much love from my friends while we danced around in that field, I'd still felt a tiny little bit self-conscious inside. But I'd finally come to realize something very important: You will never, ever be able to please everyone. It's impossible. There will always be people who don't like you or what you do. It sucks, but it's true. And honestly, who would even want to live in a world where everyone loved the same things? It sounds like kind of a boring place to me.

Once I started to look at things in that context, I realized it didn't matter one single atom's worth of thought what another person's opinion of me was. I have a seriously blessed life.

At the end of the day the only person whose opinion matters when it comes to you is *yourself*. I don't mean that in an "always look out for number one" kind of way. I mean that you'll never be able to reach your full potential if you waste time looking at how you interact with the world from someone else's perspective. As long as you follow the golden rule (you know, do unto others, etc.), nothing else should matter.

Finally letting go of that last remaining bit of self-doubt was so freeing that I knew I had to celebrate. Publicly.

Right after VidCon I recorded a cover of "Really Don't Care" that Charlie Puth produced for me, and Shelby and I hit the streets of Los Angeles. The idea was that I'd go up to total strangers and start dancing next to them while singing the song. And ideally the person or persons would dance with me, but you know what? If they didn't, I REALLY DIDN'T CARE!!

We drove everywhere, from Venice Beach to Santa Monica to Hollywood Boulevard. Shelby filmed me going up to strangers and dancing my butt off in front of them. No big surprise here, but teenagers were the most responsive. I got some professional break-dancers involved at one point and did my best to keep up. My favorite was when I convinced someone dressed up as a gorilla to get down with me. Oh, and apparently I danced up on some members of a massively famous Korean pop group called BTS, but I never realized it.

I'd say overall that the reactions were split about 50/50. Half the people looked at me like I was insane before slowly backing away, and the other half would dance along with me. I think I might have gotten a higher dance participation percentage if we'd had the music blasting, but all we had was this tiny speaker that you could barely hear anything out of, especially if the street was crowded. So a lot of the time it just seemed like I was dancing to nothing. I think those instances were when we got the most people to run away from us. Those were also the moments when I most felt my new power of not caring soar. Even just a few months earlier I probably would have felt a twinge of disappointment or embarrassment if someone sneered at me, but not the new Ricky.

New Ricky didn't give a what.

CHALLENGE

#PUBLICDANCEFORRICKY

Make a video of yourself

dancing in public.

CONCLUSION

Well, that's it, for now. Emphasis on "for now." So much has changed in my life just in the time it took to write this book, so who knows what's next? I shot a short film, I released an album, I made several music videos for it, I posted a new video every day for a month last December, and I traveled to Hawaii and Japan (I almost made it to Paris, but got diverted due to a security issue). I swam with sharks, took a dip into a volcano, booked a national tour with Trevor, and moved into a new apartment right down the street from Connor. If I took a minute to stop and think about it all, I might actually get exhausted. Better to keep on moving.

You want to know the *real* reason I decided to write a book that was full of challenges? It's still definitely because I want to follow along with all of you and have us do fun projects together, but I have to confess I had another motive. I've been so incredibly lucky and blessed to get to do the things I've done in my life, and I want everyone to experience new things in theirs, too. Getting up off your butt and putting yourself out there is the only way to learn who you are and grow into the best person you can become. Sometimes that involves picking up a book, or a camera, or a microphone, or a pencil or paintbrush. *All* the time it means not being scared to try new things, and never being ashamed of who you are. It means learning from mistakes and putting the pieces in place to make your dreams come true. Life itself is the ultimate challenge, and I know that every one of you can ace it.

Another big reason for the challenges is that I've learned life is all about connectivity. It's my biggest hope that by sharing all of the tags in here as you make your way through the book you'll get to meet new people and start conversations. Maybe you'll find a new best friend, or someone to date, or a person who five years from now will be sitting on the other side of the desk when you walk into a job interview. Our common ground doesn't just bond us—it builds us.

Okay, maybe I'm getting a little too philosophical here. I'll reel it back in. The *most* important thing is to get creative with this book and just have fun. Interacting with all of you as we do these challenges together, I know I will.

Love,
Ricky

ACKNOWLEDGMENTS

Thank you first and foremost to God. I'm so blessed and forever grateful to be able to live the life that I live. It's so important to me to be a good example and role model for people, so I always hope I'm doing just that.

To my family: Thank you, all of you, for the unconditional love and support for everything I do. Mom and Dad, I'm so blessed and grateful to have such incredible and supportive parents. I wouldn't be the person I am today without everything you've taught me growing up. Tara, thank you for being the best sister I could ever ask for and for being my role model growing up. I truly believe I got through so many things as a kid and teenager because I had someone like you to look up to. And to the rest of my family—my cousins, aunts, uncles, and grandparents—thank you all, as well, for the amazing love and support. It always makes me so happy to see you supporting my career.

To Shelby: Thank you for being the absolute best friend I could ever ask for. You've been with me through everything! Friends come and go, and it's sad to lose touch with friends from high school, but that isn't the case with us. I'm so grateful to have had you as a best friend for so long. I don't think I would have gotten through so many things if it wasn't for you. You're literally my rock. I'm so lucky to have you as my go-to person for nearly anything and everything. I can't picture my life at all without you. I can't wait for the future because I know you'll be a huge part of it!

To the O2L guys—Connor, Jc, Kian, Sam, and Trevor: The O2L channel may be over but you guys will always be such a huge part of my life. I love how we're still such good friends even after O2L. O2L aside, you guys are some of my best friends. We've always said we are all more like brothers, which is so true to me. Thanks for being such a huge part of my story and having such a huge impact on my life! I wouldn't want to have had the experiences I've had with you all with anyone else. I can't wait for even more craziness with you guys in the future.

To all my other friends from YouTube: It's weird for me to call you "YouTube friends," because at this point in my life practically all of my friends are from YouTube—haha. Jenn, Andrea, Jack, Andrew, Rebecca, Anthony, Colleen, Mikey, Luke, Lia, Drew, Alexa, Shane, and so, so many more. Honestly, I'm so lucky to have the number of amazing friends I have. I wish I could sit here and list all of you. Thank you for being such awesome people in my life! The coolest part about the YouTube community is how supportive and friendly everyone is. I love the community so much and am so grateful to be a part of it. It's changed my life.

To my incredible manager and business partner, Andrew Graham: I don't even know where to begin, but thank you for everything. I count one of the biggest turning points my career when we met and started working together. You'v been such an incredible manager and friend to me and always pushed me to be the best me I can be. There were so many times where I truly don't think I would have survived if it wasn't for you. Thank you for having such a huge and positive impact on my life so far. I can't wait to work with you even more in the future!

To my amazing producer and music mentor, Bobby: I'm so glad we started working together because you have dramatically changed and helped my music career in such a positive way. I'm so excited for what the future will bring.

To my awesome director, Andrew Vallentine: Literally all of my best and favorite videos I've ever made are thanks to you. I love working with you and honestly can't picture myself working with other directors because you're just so perfect for me! I can't wait to continue creating with you!

And to the rest of my team behind the scenes, thank you all so much for keeping me sane—haha. The adult/real world is hard and scary, and the biggest reason why I get through it is because I'm surrounded by such a phenomenal team of people.

And lastly, thank you, Joshua Lyon, for helping me create this book. You were such a joy and pleasure to work with. Also, thanks to my awesome and hardworking team at Keywords Press/Simon & Schuster: Rakesh Satyal, Judith Curr, Peter Borland, Ariele Fredman, Jackie Jou, and Jin Yu. You guys are the best, and it's been such a pleasure to work with you all! Thank you for your patience with me as we worked on the book in the midst of my crazy schedule and life! We made something pretty awesome here that I will cherish for the rest of my life.